Nurturing Your Child's Spirit

A Montessorian Approach

Jeannine L. Schmid, Ph.D.

T R E E H A U S

Treehaus Communications, Inc. P.O. Box 249, Loveland, OH 45140

To my mother and father, to the church

Nihil Obstat:
Austin B. Vaughan, S.T.D.
Censor Lihororum

Imprimatur:
Terence J. Cooke, D.D.
Archbishop of New York
May 3, 1968

Book design by Susan E. Jackson Dowd

First Edition, 1969
Second Edition, 1970
Third Edition, 1997

© Copyright 1969, 1970 by Benzinger, Inc.
© Copyright 1997 by Treehaus Communications, Inc.

Library of Congress Catalog Number 68–56936
Manufactured in the United States of America
ISBN 1-886510-10-5

Art by the children of the Laureate School in lessons designed by Sandra Kay Johnson, MFA. This lesson focuses on the growth of a seed by flowing water.
Art credits:
Cover, ix, xii, xv, xviii, 1: Jonathan Eidson
10: Brianna Stansel
Cover, 17, 120, 123: Nicholas Pruit
20: Amanda Gilbert
27: Mattie Bishop
Cover, 33: Jacqueline Davis
Cover, 40: Alex Cegelski
49: Allysa Rueschenberg
58: Thomas Worger
64: Jacob Hendricks
76: Mackenzie Anderson
84, 97: Tyler Brown
101, 110, 117: Jolyon Johnson

Contents

Preface to the Third Edition   ix

Preface to the Second Editon   xii

Preface to the First Edition   xv

Introduction   xviii

1. The Human Religious Development of the Young Child   1

    Human Development of the Child   1
    Stages of Emotional Development   2
    Stages of Intellectual Development   4
    Emotional and Intellectual Development and Religion   5

2. The Montessori Method and Religious Education   10

    Maria Montessori's Life   10
    Maria Montessori's Method   11
    The Montessori Classroom   12
    Religious Possibilities of the Montessori Classroom   13

3. Religion, Montessori, and the Home   17

    The Home as a Prepared Environment   17
    The Parent as Observer   18

4. Symbolism   20

   Conventional and Natural Symbols   20
   Prepared Environment   21
   The Tree Symbol   21

5. Cosmic, Psychological, and Social Symbols   27

   Levels of Symbolism   27
   Development of the Symbolism System   27
   The Teacher's Attitude   28
   The Symbolism of Water   29

6. Principles of Teaching   33

   Method of Teaching   33
   Order of Presenting a Lesson   34
   The Symbolism of the Rock   35

7. Discipline and Silence   40

   Discipline   41
   The Deviated Child   41
   Establishment of Discipline   43
   The Silence Game   44
   The Symbolism of Light   45

8. The Sensitive Periods   49

   The Sensitive Periods   49
   Child Development in the Home   50
   The Symbolism of the Seed   50

9. Education of the Senses   58

   Sensory Education   58
   Creation of Order and Clarity in Sense Impressions   58
   Selection of Proper Materials   59
   The Symbolism of the Table   59

10. Religious Psychology of the Child   64

    Religious Realities   64
    Religious Psychology of the Young Child   66
    Christ the Risen Lord   67

11. Children and the Liturgy   76

    Language and the Three-Period Lesson   76
    The Word in Our Faith   77
    The Symbolism of the Word   77

12. Liturgy and Celebration   84

    Liturgy   84
    Community   86
    Singing in Community   87
    Breaking Bread in Community   87
    A Celebration for Children   89

13. Conclusion   97

    Foundations for Religious Education   97
    Montessori's Principles   98
    The Lord's Supper   99

Appendix I
The Child and the Sacrament of Penance   101

    Psychology of the Young Child   103
    Religious Education and Formation of Conscience   105
    Some Practical Suggestions
        for the Guidance of the Young Child   106
        The Use of Religious Sentiments   106
        The Meaning of Words   107
        The Meaning of the Sign of Obtaining Forgiveness:
            The Sacrament of Penance   107

Appendix II
The Preschool Religious Class   110

    Advantages of the Formal Classroom   110
    Requirements for the Classroom   111
    The Preschool Religion Teacher   111
    Schedule for a Preschool Religious Class   114
    The Classroom Setting   115

Appendix III
The Mentally Challenged and Non-English Speaking Children   117

Bibliography   120

About the Author   123

Preface to the Third Edition

This preface is being written from California twenty-seven years after the publication of the first edition. Like most Californians I am not from California. Unlike Winnie the Pooh, I came here not looking for a pot of honey, but carrying one full of the riches of experiences and gifts others have given to me.

My life began in St. Paul, Minnesota, as the fifth child in a German Catholic family of ten. That family, amidst the harsh Minnesota winters, put into my honey pot a "can do" spirit. At the age of eighteen, after I was graduated from St. Joseph Academy, I joined the religious community of the Glenmary Home Mission Sisters in Cincinnati, Ohio. Their youthful leadership and extraordinary love of the poor of the Appalachian mountains gave me a deep sense of community and commitment.

The Adrian Dominicans from Siena Heights College welcomed some of us Glenmary Sisters to attend their college and I earned a bachelor of arts with a major in English literature in Adrian, Michigan. I dragged my honey pot from there to Greenwich, Connecticut, to study the Montessori Method under the leadership of Nancy McCormick Rambusch, founder of the American Montessori Society. It was there that I was given the benefit of learning the philosophical foundations of American education and how Montessori's philosophy complemented it. I learned that I, too, was a pragmatist because I was happy to receive two diplomas, one signed by Mario Montessori, who succeeded his mother as the European leader and the other by Mrs. Rambusch, president of the newly formed American group. This was 1963. Earlier I had taught for three years in a parochial school, with summer training in Cincinnati. I knew just enough to sense as so many others had that Montessori's method held great promise for education in the United States.

Little did I realize that my Winnie the Pooh odyssey had hardly begun. At that time the Montessori group in Chicago as well as groups in other places were calling for an application of the Montessori principles to the theology that emerged after Vatican II. I tried to imitate Maria Montessori's approach to designing a curriculum by studying theology and trying out "lessons" with preschool children in a Montessori classroom. Alcuin Montessori School hired me to do that and weekly I traveled from Oak Park, Illinois, to Marquette University in Milwaukee to study theology in the department headed by Dr. Bernard Cooke. He graciously answered the questions of this Montessori teacher and I began to see the connection between sacramental theology and the nurturance these signs and symbols give to children in everyday life. My master's thesis was based on that premise and eventually became this book.

When I left the Glenmary community in 1966, I took in my brimming pot a love for the poor and a sense of community. A group of us lived at the bottom of Price Hill, a rundown area of Cincinnati. There I found a group of parents willing to start a Montessori school to serve both middle class and disadvantaged children. We called it, "Montessori Center Room," because we wanted to encourage a cultural exchange as well as support less advantaged children. Today, this school continues and has at least one second-generation child in its program.

It became time to learn how to research Montessori to distinguish between mere assumptions and hopes to the results found in evidence and documentation. Needless to say, Maria stood up to the test. I earned a PhD at Purdue University in 1972 in child development and family life and accepted a position as a professor at Buffalo State University. One may think that the many lectures I gave dipped into my pot. If so, it kept getting replenished by the insights of so many communities of students and professors.

I was in Buffalo to experience the closing of Bethlehem Steel Company and observed and finally succumbed to the financial problems of the State of New York. Thus, in 1978, along with thirty-nine other newly hired professors, I had to grab my pot and was welcomed to California Polytechnic State University in San Louis Obispo as a temporary replacement for another professor on leave.

In this idyllic setting on the central coast of California I met both my husband, Alfred Barry Olson, and my co-partner, Laura C. Lehmann, and her husband, Dr. Basil Fiorito. Together, we opened a Montessori preschool in 1981 that grew and grew until we now have ten acres on one side of Bishop's Peak with 16,000 square feet of classrooms. The Montessori Method is the basis for the toddler to kindergarten program and the first to eighth grades use the California Frameworks, which sound as though Montessori might have helped write them.

What do all these adventures have in common? For me, the answer is community and commitment..

The school, The Laureate Private School with some 300 children, is a nonsectarian school. It is also a for-profit school, corporately, not actually. These decisions were made as a response to the community of San Luis Obispo and its environs.

The Laureate has always had a scholarship fund. In 1997 it expanded in order to provide program possibilities to children in programs not in our school. Children from Russia and Japan who come with their families to study English are attending the Laureate's after-school and summer program in a rich cultural exchange.

For sixteen years, Barry, Basil, Laura, and I have been literally building the foundation upon which the healing aspects of art and nature found in rocks, water, plants, fire, and trees can still be experienced in the nonsectarian traditions and rituals that all schools attempt to embody. We hope the children are nourished daily and go to their own churches with their parents, prepared to appreciate the beauty of tradition and the responsibilities that come with growing up.

When Gerard Pottebaum asked me about publishing a new edition of this book, I thought of the new re-releases of twenty-five-year-old films, like "Star Wars," and hoped that the words I had written at an earlier time could be relevant, too. Phrases have been changed, but I am not embarrassed about the overall content of this work. In fact, as I went through the exercise of bringing this work up to date, my "cup" is overflowing with gratitude for all the people who gave me so much. I hope that in some way, this loving community will experience in its lifelong journey the nurturance I have had.

Jeannine Schmid
June 1997

Preface to the Second Edition

I write this preface from the inner city. I write it 100 years after Maria Montessori was born. I write it three years after I wrote the first preface and ask myself the question, "How much do I retract of what I had first written?" My first preface was written from the inner city also, but now it is some time later, and I have been intensively involved in two worlds.

One world contains people struggling to survive. These people have little time to ask about the meaning of life, because they are so concerned about staying alive. The Christian message that Jesus is alive is seldom heard by them directly. Rather. they can only respond to people who can give them means to stay alive and who are interested in their future well–being. They know much of love and forgiveness but, as yet, they do not have the time to figure out whether or not this love and forgiveness may have some connection to a long tradition of people who called themselves followers of Christ. My involvement with this world of poverty has been to take the smallest children of this world and bring them into a garden of delight in which they have the freedom to find out that there are some adults whom they can trust and who can give them colors, objects, songs, and words to express and free the deep feelings within them.

Into this same garden of delight, we also brought the youngest people of another world. These children belong to what is called the middle class or upper middle class. The people of this world have time to think and wonder about the meaning of life since so many of its necessities are taken care of for them. These people are more sophisticated and can wonder about the long tradition of people who said they followed Jesus Christ and, yet, were hard–put to find these people connected directly to some of the things he stood for—concern for the poor and the rights of all. The youngest people of this world brought their trust of adults, their ability to laugh and sing, to imagine and be creative.

They even brought some of their own clothes to this inner-city world, and the garden of delight became a microcosm of the hope that we have for the future in which all people will be united in love and concern.

In the last 3 years, while helping this garden of delight to grow and expand so that there would be 2 schools and some 120 children gathered together, I have been also able to speak across the country and help people who are trying to work with Sunday School classes find ways to reach very small children and, more important, their parents. Most of these people previously had opportunities to participate in an action–orientated adult education process by becoming immersed in an experience with children, and from this experience many came to understand in a very deep and personal way some of the roots of their belief.

Often I have been asked whether or not I teach religion in my preschools. To me, this question is proof that we have not yet understood what religion is. If by religion one means a lession in time in which children are taught the rituals and formulas of belief, then I say "No, I am not teaching religion." But, if by religion one implies the deepest longing of a human personality and its effort to get to its deepest self and, thus, reach out towards others and to something that is somehow mysteriously divine, then I say "Yes, we are teaching religion in our schools every minute of the day and it also reaches into the night."

For in my small schools, set in an environment of neglect, we have had occasion to notice with the children some of the most nodal, or seminal, events in a human person's life. Does not a teacher respond when a baby is born? What does a teacher do when an older brother dies from a fall from a billboard because there is no regular playground available for him to scale and climb in? What does a teacher do when the children are excited about a fellow teacher's getting married? How does the teacher respond to the utter need for forgiveness when there are fights? Even more so, what does the teacher do when the father of one of the children is taken to jail as a suspect for murder and is finally released as innocent after three weeks of containment? All of these things are deeply religious happenings and concerns. How the teacher, the children and the parents respond can become a ritual in which we reach out toward divinity.

When responding religiously to these very seminal events, a teacher must do so through concrete things like a candle; or hands stretched out or clasped together; or a small plant that is growing; or some drink, cookie, or bread to be broken and given out. These are all elements of celebration, symbolic means of communicating something that is much deeper and beyond all of us. This teacher prepares and is able to respond properly because he or she has helped the children to see these concrete things in these deeper dimensions.

None of the lessons outlined in the following pages have been used in our schools exactly as they are written. Yet, all of the aspects of these lessons and the concrete forms that they suggest have been a part of the prepared environment of the classroom and have been acceptable to the children. Most of all, they have been a part of our parties.

We had a party when one of our teachers had to resign because she was going to have a baby. The children thought the baby was going to be born at the party. That really would have been the most appropriate thing to have happened! Yet, the children celebrated the baby's coming, and at the picnic at the end of the school year they happily gathered around the new baby. For them, this event was a true experience of community. They had a part in helping this baby begin to sense love.

This is the meaning of community. This is why we, as Christians, say Jesus is alive. We do not tell people that Jesus is alive so that they can conjure in their imagination the presence of some invisible person who is always around ready to give a helping hand, especially in impossible situations. Rather, we believe in the Easter mysteries because we experience the love we have among one another, a love that is somehow more divine while at the same time being very human. Hope for us becomes personalized, because we know Jesus is alive.

Young children are sensitive to such a mystery mostly because they are very animistic. They love the impossible and the mysterious, and we must be ever so careful to let them know that what we are speaking about is not an invisible personage, but the experience we have of one another that becomes so divine in its inexplicable otherness.

When we become very interior and listen to our deepest self we find that our deepest selves go beyond ourselves and as we believe, we find God—for us the risen Christ. One is only able to do this insofar as one has been called from oneself through others. This is what one might call the cosmic Jesus. Children experience this, but they are not yet ready to make a mature commitment to this mystery. However, children must be given some words for their experience, they must have language, they must be paid attention to and that is the purpose of our work.

I should also like to add some comments concerning this work and its relationship to mentally challenged children and non–English speaking children. Questions have been asked concerning these areas and we will deal with them in Appendix III.

Again, I would like to express my gratitude for the many, many people who have worked with the material that we have here represented and have thus given life to something beyond mere prose.

Jeannine Schmid
Easter 1970

Preface to the First Edition

A large female South Sea turtle comes up from the water onto an island and deposits her eggs inland. After a rest, she begins to search for the way back to the water. She crawls in an aimless fashion over the island, trying one direction and then another; yet she cannot find the water from which she has crawled. The turtle has lost her sense of direction because the water for which she searches has been contaminated by poisonous fallout from underwater tests conducted by humans who have been trying to discover a more effective bomb. Finally, after days spent circling the island, the turtle dies. A whitened shell among many other whitened shells remains.

This is one scene from a 1963 movie called *Mondo Cane*. Many who watched the turtle saw her plight as a symbol of the loss of direction that is the legacy of the modern world.

The basic questions about the existence and direction of humanity are being asked now with a greater urgency than ever before. The answers to these questions cannot be the same as they once were. There must be a more radical answer to the problems that humanity faces, because we find ourselves in the most terrifying situation of all times. The late Abraham J. Heschel, a Jewish philosopher and theologian, stated that questions we seriously ask today would have seemed utterly absurd twenty years ago. He cited these questions in his book, *Who Is Man?* (Stanford University Press, Stanford, Calif.): "Are we the last generation? Is this the very last hour for western civilization?" If these are today's questions, what will the person of the future ask? What questions will the four-year-old child be asking twenty years from now? Such considerations lead us to believe that today we must seek a more radical approach to the education of the young child. No longer can we use the same words or the same techniques, nor can we exhibit the same attitudes. We can no longer speak of a teacher–classroom technique in the traditional sense, and we cannot speak of a "series of lessons" for a child.

This book proposes to help parents and teachers to understand and to observe the growth of a child within the child's own home environment during the child's years of existence. It proposes to develop an attitude concerned, not with lessons about life, but with celebrations of life. It suggests that parents and teachers look with the child at things that say life, in order that those who celebrate—mother, father, teacher, child—may exist in peace. It is only in discovering a technique of becoming that we may be assured of a sense of direction.

It seems proper, then, to begin our discussion by placing it in the broader context of the church and the world of human society. After all, unless children see themselves in relation to the world in which they live, they will not be truly educated. The opening words of *The Constitution on the Church in the Modern World* state:

The joys and the hopes, the griefs and the anxieties of the men of this age, especially those who are poor or in any way afflicted, these are the joys and hopes, the griefs and anxieties of the followers of Christ . . . For the human person deserves to be preserved; human society deserves to be renewed (par. 1 & 3).

What good will it do to teach a child to say the name of Jesus reverently if we do not stress that we are brothers and sisters in Jesus? What good will it do to sing songs with children if there is little or no connection between the songs and the world in which these children sing? What purpose will it serve to say anything to little children about God if what is said in the parish church is not said at home; or if what is said in one parish church is not said in another; and more, what is said by one denomination is not said by another? The church, the community, the world—all must speak the same thing to each other. Christ said, "What I say to you in the dark, tell it in the light; and what you hear whispered, proclaim from the housetops" (Matt. 10:27).

Perhaps this means that what is whispered in darkness must be able to be proclaimed from the housetops. This is the task of every adult, especially those who teach children; it is the task of the church. What we tell our children now is not to be discarded when they grow up. It must grow with them as they grow in the world and become a part of the world.

The message of Christianity is such that it can be spoken in all places and at all times to all people at all stages of their development. The task before the church today is to speak this "good news" in such a way that all people in all places can understand it. What is the key message of Christianity? It is this: Christ is risen from the dead.

This is the word that the apostles gave the people after the Spirit came to them on Pentecost. The apostles spoke about Christ's life and death because they knew that he was alive and in their very midst. Their main concern was that everyone should know that Jesus is alive. They knew what their task in the world was when they realized that Jesus was not dead. They knew this most profoundly when they gathered together and celebrated his existence in their midst with great thanksgiving. St. Paul, who knew Christ only as One who was risen and in his midst, exhorted his people as he exhorts us today—to remember that whenever we are together we are proclaiming this same message. We proclaim this message in our gatherings until Christ comes.

Does this make sense in the world in which we live today? Christ is risen. Does this message fit the way we live? Yes, because the message is concerned with life, and life is surrounded with signs that speak of it. There are natural signs, such as water or a rock, which remind us that we thirst or that we need protection. There are signs such as a gesture of greeting, which remind us of love, acceptance, and joy. All these signs point to life, and all can point to eternal life—risen, unlimited life. One of the ways through which we can be led to know Christ is through an understanding of these signs, for Christ is the fullness of life. Christ is water springing up. Christ is a rock of fidelity. Christ reaches out to us in a gesture of love and healing.

These signs are important for Christians not only because they remind us of Christ, but because we actually know and come to Christ through some of these things: through water and a gesture of welcome at Baptism, for example. Christ took many natural things and many human gestures and made them the means through which we can know him and come into union with him. These means are what we now know as the seven sacraments.

The sacraments are made up of the signs of life. We must learn to read these signs. When we do, we have the opportunity to become totally involved with Christ and, through him, with all people.

This study could not have been undertaken without the encouragement and advice of many people. The existence of this book is attributable to a number of people. To list individuals would be impossible. Yet, we must express gratitude to Earl Johnson and Bernard Cooke, and to Nancy McCormick Rambusch for theological and pedagogical guidance, and to Maureen O'Connor for editing the manuscript. Perhaps the best way to thank the many others is to name them collectively as they are—members of Christ, the church.

Jeannine Schmid
Easter, 1967

Introduction

The first point we wish to make concerning this book is content: "What do I teach? Do I teach the life of Christ and the actions of God in the Bible; the Christian life of love; the creed? We want to teach all these things, but from the point of view of sacraments. If we are concerned with helping children understand the world and its deepest possible meaning, then we must help them to read the signs of life in the world, in the sacraments. Then they will know their relationship with Christ, themselves, the world, and all others. What we are especially speaking about now are the signs of water, oil, bread, and community. These signs in the sacraments tell us and give us Christ who satisfies our thirst and gives us healing, nourishment, and love.

Thus, we suggest that every child be helped to look around and see what the world is saying. This means that everyone who teaches must try to understand the meaning of these signs. What does bread say to us about the Eucharist, and what does the Eucharist say about the world? What can flowers, rocks, water, and other signs say about our relationship with God? In this book, we hope to show you and to help you to begin to show young children.

If the first consideration is content, the second is method: How do I teach a child? The young child, after all, does not have a sense of history. Do I tell the child something that happened a long time ago? The child is concerned about things that can be tasted, seen, heard and touched. How do I make the child aware of the abstract notions of sorrow, love, fidelity? First, remember that we are teaching the child about someone who is risen and alive now. This is the message of Christianity. Christ is alive and in our midst, and we want to be able to recognize him especially in the breaking of the bread, the Eucharist. Second, recall that the way to teach this great reality is to give the child an opportunity to discover it in an atmosphere of freedom, spontaneity, and conversation. It is not that we have something to tell the child that he or she is to learn, but that we have something to look at with the child. Together, we can come to understand the meaning of life for the Christian.

In the following pages, we shall unfold many principles involved in teaching the young child that were learned from studying and teaching the Montessori approach to learning.

The plan of this book follows the manner in which we experimented. When we worked with children, we did not plan our lessons ahead of time. We observed how a certain sign had something to say to us and the children, and then presented it to the children. These lessons, then, are not arranged chronologically, nor need they be. The basic truth symbolized by water, for instance, does not necessarily have to precede the basic truth that is found in the symbol of the rock. It does not matter which comes first. What is important is that we begin to look around with our children and try to understand what is being said to us in our everyday lives. Thus, instead of first discussing the Montessori Method and then trying to apply it to religious ideas, we feel that it would be more in keeping with our everyday life and more in the spirit of this experiment to consider one method at a time, and keep it in mind as we discover, discuss, or delight with the child about an aspect of everyday life that speaks of the person of Christ and of his relationship to the world. In this way the techniques that Maria Montessori suggested may be learned more through practice than through theory.

Chapters 1 and 2 of this book describe the human religious development of the young child, and the Montessori Method and religious education. Chapter 3 deals with religion, Montessori, and the home. Chapters 4 through 12 present one of Maria Montessori's insights, and includes a presentation of a biblical image that is also a sign of Christ's presence to the world. In addition, these chapters suggest how parents may learn this with their child. In Appendices I and II we discuss the child and Penance and describe for teachers of preschool religion classes ways in which the suggestions in this book may be used in a classroom situation.

What do we hope to accomplish by this approach to the young child? This question can only be answered by each person who is in relationship with a child. However, we hope that we can help our children to become more human by helping them to respect and reverence all that is in the world. We hope that children can then begin to sense that it is through the world that they will understand the presence of a person who is the answer to all of life. We also hope that they will come to the words of the Bible with an understanding born of an experience of the meaning of the images presented there. These same biblical words will be part of the worship experience of life when, as adults, they gather with other Christians. We therefore hope that we are presenting here basic forms, basic elements of true liturgy, for there are certain gestures, songs, and images that are a part of the effort to ritualize the yearnings of every person's heart.

It would be well to ask at this point, "Why should we consider religious education for the young child?" Perhaps an even more basic question should be asked, "Why should we consider education for the young child at all?" When we speak of the young child we mean the child of two, three, and four years of age. It is interesting to note that the more we understand the young child as personality grows and develops from the first moments of consciousness, the more we can understand ourselves and others. It is only in knowing our roots that we can understand ourselves and it is only in understanding ourselves that we can understand others. Perhaps this is why the child today is of such interest to psychologists, sociologists, and theologians.

We cannot, however, think in terms of learning about children as a selfish gain. We do not educate children in order to understand ourselves, although this is a rewarding by-product. We educate children in order to help them to begin to tap their rich potential as human personalities. When we talk about educating young children, instead of thinking about remedial reading, remedial mathematics, or remedial personality development, we can and must think of reading readiness, mathematical readiness, and personality readiness. Work of this kind must necessarily be seen from a different perspective. This perspective is taken from a study of children and their spontaneous development. If it is possible to help children grow in muscular control and coordination, and thus make it easier for them to understand the words on a printed page, or to become more creative in the use of data given to them, then it is also possible to help them to grow in their own consciousness of their relationships with others and with the world. We thus make it possible for them to begin to understand the greatest and most profound meaning the world has to give. This is our concern for children—that they grow in their ability to come into relationship with others and thus into relationship with God.

The Human-Religious Development of the Young Child

A recurring question in a study such as this should be, "Why should we consider religious education for the young child?" In his book *Your Growing Child and Religion*, R. S. Lee says that when he is asked by parents about religious education for their young children, he usually shocks them by saying, "Parents, give your children as little religious instruction as possible, until they are over seven." What he is saying is, there is a difference between religious education and religious development. Religious education involves a technique of teaching beliefs and practices. Religious development, on the other hand, is what the child becomes. Religious education for the young child is most properly, then, the science of religious development. The task is to find a technique for becoming. If religious education is understood in this way, then the task of parents is not so much to respond to a child's questions with metaphysical answers such as, "God made the world"; "God is a Supreme Being," but rather to speak in terms of the child's real question: "Who in the world is for me?" Perhaps we can turn to the child and in understanding his or her quest to become a person, we can say, "I am for you. I know of someone who is for you because he is someone for me."

HUMAN DEVELOPMENT OF THE CHILD

In order to better understand how to speak in this way with a child, it is necessary to understand who the human person is. Then we can discuss the stages of development of young children before the age of six, both in their emotional and intellectual development. This awareness of the nature and development of the person leads to an understanding of religious development.

The human person is one who acts through his or her nature. In the nature of such a person there is a power consisting of human intellect and will. In order to understand the operations and functions of a person, we often speak of human intellect and will. Unfortunately, we sometimes "split" persons so that they are either thinking or willing, and we fail to see that these two features are so interconnected that one can hardly think in terms of a person's thinking, without considering feeling. So, when we consider an individual, it is better to think not so much of what, but who. When we meet someone, we do not analyze that person's thoughts or will, but rather who the person is. He or she is good, kind, does things. We think of another person not so much in terms of isolated activities, but in terms of how actions are related to something else. To be a person one must be "related." The power to think and to will can only exist in relationship to something else. Thus, a person becomes more of a person by thinking and willing in terms of someone or something else. The powers of person only "become" through communication.

It is important to think of the individual as a person only insofar as that person is able to communicate. The power that the person has must touch someone else. Usually, when we think of communication we think about talking. But what is within a person is given to another not only through the words that are spoken but through eyes and gestures. A person communicates with others by using the entire body. Accordingly, the better a person understands all of the body, the better he or she can communicate with others. The person who has the power to think has, in reality, the power to be conscious, conscious with the whole body about what is happening. We can, therefore, think of will in a more dynamic way by saying that the person is loving. To place the "ing" at the end of the word conscious, "conscious-ing," and love, "loving," puts a person into process. This is most important when we think of the developing personality. The young child is not merely sitting around with the power to think and to will. Observation alone tells us this. Rather, the child is in relationship—moving outward toward others or inward upon self. Since we are concerned with a technique for becoming, our aim is to understand how it is that the human personality develops and becomes a related personality. As we said before, in order for a person to be, that person must be related.

STATES OF EMOTIONAL DEVELOPMENT

It is important to understand the relational aspects of the human personality by first studying the three stages of the emotional development of the child, and then by observing how the child develops intellectually. We shall then try to see how emotional and intellectual development are actually a religious development.

The first three stages of emotional development, according to Erik Erikson in *Childhood and Society*, are the sense of basic trust, the sense of basic autonomy, and the sense of basic initiative. During the first two years of a child's life, foundations are laid for a sense of basic trust. It is at this time that the child learns how to receive. The manner in which the child is fed, the number and quality of feedings, condition the child for learning to trust. If the child has good experiences in receiving food in a calm and peaceful manner when it is needed, then the child is given reason to trust others. Successful in receiving what is needed, the child can now trust in the self, because of being able to trust in the mother. How is the father involved in this? The mother can supply this basic experience of trust to the child only if she feels secure herself. It is the love of the father for the mother that provides this security. So the secure atmosphere that gives a person reason to trust a situation, rather than to mistrust it, comes in these first two years of life. The parents can give this sense of trust to the child only if they have faith in themselves, and they can achieve this only insofar as they have faith in others, which is the source of faith in God.

The second stage of development, the sense of basic autonomy, comes in the next two years of life, between the ages of two and four. At this stage, the child is learning how to control and let go of the bowels. This is the toilet-training time that has been much discussed. Parents have been warned to be careful not to make children ashamed of themselves as they are learning bowel control. Actually, insofar as children can learn how to hold on and how to let go, can they learn to become the kind of persons who can be independent or autonomous. This independence is hard won. Children must learn that they can neither hold on too tightly to an idea, nor let go too soon. The parallel to the control of the bowels is obvious. Children at this age are becoming producers. We must look upon this as something that should be learned with a certain amount of self-esteem so children do not lose confidence in themselves. Children will have a sense of their own selves only insofar as they learn this task of controlling and letting go in the proper manner. They can do this with dignity if they are in relationship to parents who are aware of their own dignity.

It is in the next stage that children learn to develop a sense of basic initiative. This phase occurs between four and six years of age. (There is no precise time for a stage to begin or end. In reality each person develops at an individual pace.) The little four-year-old explores, puts things together, thinks up ideas. At this time the child becomes creative. Boys also become aware that they have genital organs that differ from those of little girls. This comparison, curiosity, finding out, are all a part of an investigation of the world. It is at this time that the child wants to stand apart from parents and tell them very definitely, "I am not you." This can be called the "No" stage. If parents do not understand that the child must make this break, the child will become frustrated in attempts to find out what the world is about and to become completely independent of parents. If the child is made to feel ashamed of explorations and of curiosity about the body, then the child will hold back in trying new ideas, in taking initiative. Again, the child's own basic initiative will be a reflection of the parents' ability to come to terms with the body.

When a child is deprived of the proper relationship with parents—especially with the mother—the child will evince a lack of ability to trust, to be autonomous, and to exercise initiative. John Bowlby in his book, *Child Care and the Growth of Love*, reports on a study of 102 boys between the ages of 15 and 18 who regularly broke the school rules. The study showed that their antisocial activities were traceable to poor relationships in their early childhood. In other words, children under the age of seven years are in danger of possible injury to the development of their mental health if they are deprived of warm, intimate, and constant relationships with parents. It is important that both parents realize that they, together, will form the child. They contribute according to their own personality. Both masculine and feminine influences are needed. Deprived children then are ones who lack the constant opportunities to hear words spoken to them, to feel or be able to seek the touch of their mother's body, to see the color of her eyes, skin, clothing, and then gradually relate these to the world about them. Such children may develop into persons full of anxieties, with an excessive need for love and powerful feelings of revenge.

STAGES OF INTELLECTUAL DEVELOPMENT

The development of the emotional life of the child occurs at the same time as the child's intellectual life is being developed. When we speak of knowing for children under seven, we mean that they know through their senses. This is the first step in learning. We call this perceptual learning: children learn through experience. Later on they can move away from mere sense impressions and think about what they have felt. This step is called *conceptual* learning. Children feel acceptance and love, and learn to trust and to respond to this love—they learn to love. They know love in a perceptual way. Later on they reflect this experience and say, "I have been loved." This is knowing love in a *conceptual way*.

We can speak of learning for the child under the age of five in yet another way. Instead of speaking of perceptual learning, we can say that the child is at a preoperational stage of learning. At this time the child learns by trial and error. Jerome Bruner says in his book *The Process of Education* that teachers are severely limited in transmitting concepts to a child under the age of five. The child is establishing relationships between experience and action, and is manipulating the world through action. The child is learning with his or her legs. It is at this time that a child can learn that two and two are four more easily by taking two things and putting them next to two other things. This is better than simply having the child look at two things and see that two things and two more things equal four things. This intellectual development corresponds roughly to the period of the first development of language when the child learns to represent the world through symbols. Seeing that a certain sign has a certain meaning, the child begins to generalize, and recognizes that every time this sign is seen it means the same thing. As an example, the child at first may walk in the woods and see one squirrel after another, but think of each squirrel as the same squirrel. Later on the child begins to generalize and to apply the idea of a squirrel to all squirrels.

The important task of the parent during this stage of development is to provide the child with many opportunities to manipulate the world through action. The child must be given the opportunity to explore the variety of ways to put together blocks, cardboard boxes, and other materials. The child should be given a chance to match things, to see differences, and to realize that things can be arranged in a variety of ways. The parent who is overly concerned about keeping everything in order and who is afraid to let the child touch, taste, and discover with the mouth and toes as well as with the hands, is a parent who frustrates this important concrete stage of learning. At this age, the only way the child comes to know things is by concretely experiencing them.

EMOTIONAL AND INTELLECTUAL DEVELOPMENT AND RELIGION

How do these stages of emotional and intellectual development relate to religion? Perhaps we can already see some connections. When the child is learning to identify with the mother in the first stage of trust, one may consider this love between the two, grace. Grace is the friendship of God for the child through the mother. The child's own trust and faith is a reflection of the faith of the parents, and the parents' faith is a reflection of the Christian community surrounding them and their child. The community of the church, then, has a relationship to the child from the first moments of existence. Only insofar as the community of Christians lives in a secure trust and faith can the child grow up with a basic sense of trust. At the time when the child is learning to identify with the mother and learning how to hold on and how to let go, the child makes a joyful identification with the mother's prayers. The mother, too, is learning how to hold on and let go. According to Augustine Leonard, O.P., the child has no exact representation of God in mind. But at this stage, the child becomes more personally involved with environment and endows everything with spirit. Praying is a big game and this is good. (One wonders if praying should not always be fun.) It is at this time that a feeling for the sacred is born.

A continuation of this feeling of the sacred and this endowment of everything with life is seen in the third stage of initiative. The child is really like a person from an ancient civilization, projecting feelings onto objects, or even onto imaginative playmates. The child identifies with the world in a magical way—credulous, trusting, communicative. Ignoring the impossible, the child peoples the world with angels and devils. This is the time for parents to consider carefully the words they use to explain things. It is better not to talk at all than to emphasize things that may be seen only as magical.

What are some of the implications of these insights for the teaching of religion today? If the child manipulates the world through action and through symbols, then the parent interested in giving the child a firm foundation and an ability to believe, should share with the child experiences of real symbols or real signs that speak of a personal relationship to God. Is not the child's wonder at water something that God appealed to when speaking to the ancient Hebrews? Can we not speak in the same way to a child? If the child is establishing in the mind, through trial and error, certain patterns of response to playthings, then should we not think of letting the child "play" with the words and the concrete images of our faith? What is concrete about our faith? The most concrete fact is that Jesus is alive. We are talking about life, and all about us are the signs of life that appeal to a child's sense of wonder. We do not need then, to give the child a formula stating that God is our life, anymore than we need to provide a formula stating that two and two are four. If a child learns more through a long period of discovery, then why not take the time to let the child repeat and discover over and over again the meaning of water, light, or a rock?

If the child is peopling the world with angels and devils, would it not be better to let the child look at the wonders of reality and see what is there, rather than reciting long stories about angels and devils? Instead of telling the child about the seven days of creation, why not speak of Christ as brother and God as father and mother. Remember that the child is more interested in learning how Christ is his brother and how God is a parent, than in knowing that God made all things out of nothing.

Religion is the personal relationship of a person to God. God as a parent with a constant tenderness, calls us children through acts of love, and thus acts in relationship with us. Insofar as we accept this call, we are saved. But we may ask, how can children know of this divine love? How real can this love be? In the New Testament, Philip asks in a childlike manner, "Lord, show us the Father, and we will be satisfied." The answer Christ gives to Philip is the same answer he gives us today: "Have I been with you all this time, Philip, and still you do not know me? Whoever has seen me has seen the Father" (John 14:8). Because Christ became one of us and is with us today as the head of the church, united with each of us, its members, we know the love of God for us. Yet, how does a child, who learns through sense perceptions, know of this love? St. John, in his first letter to the early Christians, answered the question in this way: "What was from the beginning, and we have heard, what we have seen with our eyes, what we have looked at and touched with our hands . . . we declare also to you" (1 John 1:1–4).

From the earliest days of Christianity, people have proclaimed the love of God because they have accepted the Son, Jesus Christ. When a mother and father love their child, they proclaim the love of God for their child. A child experiences the love of God through the love of parents. Therefore, when we say that the child's ability to know and to love, to learn and to relate depends to a great extent on a stable first seven years, we are speaking not only of an emotional and intellectual stability, but of what may be called a religious stability. God through Jesus Christ, has made it possible for us to have a personal relationship with the almighty. This is made known through Christ and is proclaimed by Christians.

Is there any other way that children can learn of God's love for them except through the excellent way of experiencing their parents' love? There is another way and this way also flows from parental love. We can have a meaningful understanding of Christ and relationship to us by looking at and experiencing the things of nature. St. Paul, in writing to the Romans, said, "Ever since the creation of the world his (God's) eternal power and divine nature, invisible though they are, have been understood and seen through the things he made" (Rom. 1:20). The creation of the world demonstrates to us the love of God.

Yet we live in the twentieth century, far removed from the days of St. Paul. Are these things of nature still speaking to us? Look at an ordinary kitchen. It contains a table about which we sit to eat, a faucet for water; perhaps there is an ivy plant growing along the side of the window; for certain occasions there is a candle on the table. These are the same things that were spoken of by St. Paul and St. John to those early Christians who broke bread at a table, who were baptized with water, who realized that they were one with Christ as branches are one with the vine, and who experienced the Light that had come into their darkness.

CONCLUSION

In this chapter, we have tried to see how the emotional and intellectual development of the young child is related to the development of personality in such a way that we can truly say that insofar as a person is human, that person is religious. But the question still remains: "How can my four-year-old see this as I see it?" There is an approach to teaching children that can help us begin to bring this about. We call this way the Montessori Method. In the next chapter, we will speak of Maria Montessori and her method, and try to see how it is related to religious education.

SUGGESTED READINGS

Books

Bowlby, John. *Child Care and the Growth of Love*. Baltimore, Md.: Penguin Books, 1953. (See especially Chapters 1, 2, and 3.)

Bruner, Jerome S. *The Process of Education*. New York: Vintage, 1960. (See especially Chapter 3.)

Erikson, Erik. *Childhood and Society*. New York: W. W. Morton and Co., 1963. (See especially Chapter 7.)

Lee, R. S. *Your Growing Child and Religion*. New York: Macmillan, 1963. (See especially Chapter 1.)

Robinson, John A. T. *The New Reformation*. Philadelphia: Westminster Press, 1965. (See especially Appendix II, "Spiritual Education in a World Without Religion," by Ruth Robinson.

Articles

Leonard, Augustine, O.P. "Human Religious Development of the Child," *Lumen Vitae* (1957), #2.

Pines, Maya. "A Baby's Mind: The Crucial First Months," *McCalls* (April 1967), pp. 74, 140–142.

2 The Montessori Method and Religious Education

Up to this point we have spoken of the developing human personality and examined first, what it means to be a person, and, second, the stages of development of the young child. We have done so in order to understand the task facing the parent or the teacher who wishes to educate a child. We tried to see the implications of this information for religious values and intimated that the Montessori Method would provide some practical suggestions for what may be called "a technique for becoming." We said that the child is a conscious and loving individual who can come into proper relationship with the self, the world, and God only through what Maria Montessori called an "immersion in experience." Although this entire book is devoted to a description of the Montessori Method and its applications to the religious education of the young child, in this chapter we will take time to speak about Maria Montessori and her method in a more generalized way in order to see how some of her insights, such as "ground rules" and "control of error," fit into the method she devised. We will first describe Maria Montessori as a woman in time, then, make a general statement about her Method, and, finally, relate this Method to religious education.

MARIA MONTESSORI'S LIFE

Maria Montessori was born at Chiarsvalle, Italy, in the province of Ancona, on August 31, 1870. In 1896 she became the first woman in Italy to receive a degree in medicine and surgery. During her first ten years as a doctor, she began to work with diseases of children. Her first interest was the training of "deficient children" and she began to organize, under Dr. Guido Bacelli, a training course for teachers in the education of these children. It was not until 1906, however, that the techniques she devised were applied to other children. It was in this year that she opened the first "children's house" in a slum district of Rome. Here she applied the insights of two French psychologists, Dr. Jean Itard, and his pupil, Edward Seguin, as set forth in their book, The Hygiene and Treatment of Idiot Children, in 1848. She applied to other children the scientific principles used by these men.

Dr. Seguin's physiological method with its teaching apparatus (today they would be called manipulatives) was applied to children of all kinds with such success that a new way of teaching was discovered. In 1912, six years after Maria Montessori opened her first school for "normal" children as they were thought of, she published her first book describing her work. Called *The Montessori Method*, this book applied scientific pedagogy to child education in "the children's houses." The book was followed by more books and articles that were translated almost immediately and published around the world.

Although Maria Montessori was influenced most by the French psychologists Itard and Seguin, it is interesting to note that her own discoveries were made at the time when Freud, who died in 1939, and his pupil, Adler, who died in 1937, were making great discoveries concerning the unconscious mind. Montessori was also a contemporary of John Dewey who developed his own philosophy of education in the United States. Dewey and Montessori met and discussed their work. Both died in the same year, 1952. Today, we see how closely the work of Maria Montessori paralleled that of John Dewey. Both were interested in learning through experience. But, while John Dewey was a philosopher of learning through experience, Maria Montessori was its practitioner. Finally, it is noteworthy that Maria Montessori made her contribution to education at the same time that Dr. Carl Jung, a pupil of Freud, was discovering the hidden resources of the unconscious. It is not apparent in Maria Montessori's books that she was influenced by this psychological school. However, the insights of these men into some of the symbols that we wish to apply to religious education can be easily used within the Montessori Method.

MARIA MONTESSORI'S METHOD

One way to describe the Montessori Method is to give a short definition of it: "The Montessori Method is the observation by the adult of the spontaneous development of children toward normality in a prepared environment, and the appropriate facilitation of the learning process." (This definition comes from a glossary of Montessori terms, compiled in 1962, by Nancy McCormick Rambusch, Reginald C. Orem, and George L. Stevens.) It is important to remember that in the Montessori Method the development of the child takes place under the careful observation of an adult. Montessori said, "Observation is a form of pedagogy." She placed the child in a "prepared environment," which was a "calm, ordered, protective milieu, with carefully graded stimuli (apparatus) designed to elicit from the child spontaneous involvement in a learning process." The teacher was to act as an observer as the child walked about in this specially prepared classroom and chose his or her own work.

From this careful observation, the teacher could discover how to help the child to learn. When Maria Montessori spoke about the "normalized child," she was characterizing the child who was able to fix his attention on a given piece of work, to persevere at this work, and to repeat it. Having been motivated to do this, the child would be able to focus on real learnings. All the teaching materials that Montessori used were designed to elicit from the child the ability to discern size, color, form, order, texture, sound, number, and other qualities.

THE MONTESSORI CLASSROOM

Imagine a child walking into a large room filled with furniture of a Lilliputian size. There are, as one kindergarten teacher exclaimed, "so many pots and pans around!" There is open space where children are working on rugs and, a selection of small tables and chairs. This classroom has no assigned place for the teacher's desk. In fact, it is difficult for the visitor to find the teacher because he or she may be any place in the room. Perhaps the teacher is on the floor with one or two children working on a puzzle map of the world, or at the side of a little girl at her table, looking with her at her work and showing her how to do it, or working with her.

One can see a little boy at work in the "practical life" area of the room, where he is getting water to wash dishes, or to scrub clothes or a table. Small mops, dust pans, and other household items are neatly placed within the child's reach. The child is performing these ordinary household tasks, not in order to help his mother to keep her home cleaner, but to learn motor control and coordination, an essential step in learning to read and write.

In another corner of the room, a child is occupied with a teaching apparatus designed to help understand mathematics. Another area of the room is arranged for language exercises where matching cards and learning the names of objects are two ways to promote reading readiness. Finally, a fourth area of the room has materials designed to help development of the senses. For example, bottles with various odors, are provided so that the child can compare them in order to develop a sense of smell.

How can there be a room that allows so much freedom for the child without chaos taking over? The next chapters of this book will explain in more detail how the teacher helps the child to learn discipline and to take out what is needed for work and then to put it back without disturbing other children. The ability of children to work in this way is fostered by the teacher who lays down certain necessary ground rules that bring about what Montessori called "liberty within limits." Moreover, for the first few weeks, there are no more than nine or ten children in the class at a time. More children are phased in until the class can achieve the average number of twenty-two to twenty-eight. This means that the Montessori teacher must have an assistant or two to help guide the children. The phasing-in process is most helpful because the class is made up of children between the ages of two and six. An older child, who has been in the class longer, may help and is encouraged to teach a younger child how to work in the environment. Thus, the classroom becomes a small world in which children are walking about, discovering, and working together or alone in a peaceful manner. The children are learning how to learn.

The daily schedule of a Montessori classroom is as flexible as those conducting the class wish to make it. In the United States today, many of the children attending Montessori schools have between two-and-a-half and three hours of school each day. The children arrive, greet the teacher and their classmates, and begin to work. About one-and-a-half hours later, they are asked to put their work away and to assemble for juice and cookies, or other refreshments. It is at this time that the children are introduced to the cultural refinement of eating. They learn to serve one another, to wait until all have been served before they eat. They choose to eat with each other. It is a time for them to gather together as one group and do something together. After that, depending on the observations of the teacher, some of the children may join the teacher for a special demonstration of some work in the classroom, or they may go back to their own work again. In these group sessions, the children may also sing, dance, or listen to a story.

RELIGIOUS POSSIBILITIES OF THE MONTESSORI CLASSROOM

One can easily see how a Montessori-prepared environment might be a natural place for a child to become interested in religion. If religion shows individuals how we are related to each other and ultimately to

God, then a Montessori classroom, where there is no formal attempt to teach religion, might indeed be a place where children act relationally, act religiously. The atmosphere of the classroom is one of reverence, care, and concern. This is religious.

More than that, however, in such a free environment there is the opportune time for the discovery of religious attitudes. A child may, for example, come to school with flowers. The teacher, in showing the child how to arrange the flowers in a vase of water, can, through her own attitude, give the child the opportunity for an experience of the sacred. While the teacher works with the child, other children may gather around, and together they may discover how the beauty of the flowers is a sign of life. It is perhaps at these times of incidental teaching that the teacher finds her greatest opportunities to help the child to experience the sacred. It is not so much in lectures and long explanations, but in the teacher's own attitude toward the things of the world, that the child understands there is someone beyond all of us who is for us.

Maria Montessori was interested in the religious education of the young child. When she described the child's sensitivity to color, sound, and sight, she did not neglect to mention that the child had special "religious urges." When she opened a school in Barcelona, Spain, in about the year 1919, she was able to make a more formal approach to religious education. There she experimented with a small chapel called an atrium. She supplied it with an altar and all the things that go into a church, but scaled them down to a child's size. She was interested in having the children work with all the concrete things that are used in religious services. She felt that by shining the candlesticks, arranging flowers on the altar, and filling the fonts with holy water, the child would be prepared to appreciate the experience of prayer that would take place in this small church. Her greatest insight was her realization that it was in the experience of worshiping together that people come to learn about God. Again, her philosophy was one of learning through experience. This was a great insight into liturgy for someone writing in the first quarter of the twentieth century. At that time, the liturgical renewal was just beginning. Now, some seventy years later, we have the tools to understand what makes up a liturgical, religious experience. Studies of the meaning of Scripture and the application of psychological insights to theology make it possible for us to realize that God has spoken to us in a human way. Today, therefore, we see the importance of placing side-by-side the studies of theology and anthropology. Such work furthered by outstanding theologians—Karl Rahner, for example—would have been of intense interest to a woman who wrote a book in 1913 called *Pedagogical Anthropology*.

In viewing a Montessori classroom, one understands why Maria Montessori could write in 1917, in her book *Spontaneous Activity in Education*, about the converted as one "absorbed in the contemplation of themselves in relation to a central point of their consciousness, which seems to be illuminated by some prodigious radiance." She wrote many times of the spiritual education of children. However, in the same book, in a rather obscure footnote, she states, "I cannot foresee whether I and my colleagues will be able to bring such a heavy task [the moral and religious education of children] to a successful conclusion" (ibid., page 355). It is the opinion of the present writer that Maria Montessori's greatest insight into religious education was to see it situated in the experience of worship. She did not, however, have the understanding we now have through the biblical, liturgical, and catechetical renewals, to develop these insights in the same thorough manner as she did the mathematical and sensorial training of the young child. It remains for students of Maria Montessori, who are interested in the theological insights that we have at hand today, to take the legacy of her Method and, with it, try to give to the child the possibility of an experience of the sacred.

This task of relating religious education to the Montessori Method was passed on to Montessori students through the work of E. M. Standing, who knew Maria Montessori. In 1959 he wrote the now famous book, *Maria Montessori, Her Life and Her Work*. He is also responsible for editing a book on Dr. Montessori's ideas about the religious education of children called, significantly, *The Child in the Church*. This book, first published in 1929, describes Maria Montessori's experiment in Spain. Since that time, other students of Montessori have made significant contributions to this study. One of the most notable of these is the work of H. Lubienska de Lenval, who applied the Montessori principles to her own studies of liturgical customs. To date, her only book in English is a small volume called *The Whole Man at Worship* first published in 1957.*

CONCLUSION

In this chapter, we have described briefly Maria Montessori as a woman physician who made a contribution to the world not only as a doctor but as an educator. We have tried to describe, in a general way, her method and to show how it provides the possibility for an experience of the sacred. In the next chapter, we shall see how the Montessori Method speaks to the parent and how religious education can take place in the home.

SUGGESTED READINGS

Books

de Lenval, H. Lubienska. *The Whole Man at Worship.* New York: Desclee Co., 1961. (See especially Chapter 2.)

Montessori, Maria. *Montessori Method.* New York: Schocken, 1964. (See especially Chapters 3 and 4.) ——Spontaneous Activity in Education. Cambridge: Robert Benfley, 1964.

Standing, E. M. *Maria Montessori, Her Life and Work.* New York: Mentor–Omega, 1957. (See especially Part One.)

Notes

*In a congratulatory letter from Mrs. Lubienska de Lenval written in October 1969 from Fribourg, Switzerland, I was told that there are now two more books in English. They are: *How to Teach Religion* (Chicago: Franciscan Herald Press) and *Silence in the Shadow of the World* (New York: Paulist Press).

3 Religion, Montessori, and the Home

In the first chapter, we described the development of the human personality and showed that only in a loving, warm, home relationship can a child achieve a basic sense of faith and trust. We saw that the child's faith and trust are reflections of parents' faith and trust. We can readily understand then, that the child's own religious attitudes are reflections of parents' attitudes. In Chapter 2, we described the Montessori Method and saw that the child may have the greatest opportunity for an experience of the sacred in a specially prepared environment. Now we would like to consider how all these topics are related to the home environment.

THE HOME AS A PREPARED ENVIRONMENT

The home is in every way a prepared environment. The parent is in every way a teacher who is above all an observer. The freedom and spontaneity of a home environment make it most properly a place for the experience of the sacred. If the home is "a church in miniature," then the child in the home is truly the child in the church.

Although everything in a home is not scaled to size for children, there is every reason to believe and to expect that within their own rooms children have access to all they need to care for themselves. In many homes today, parents have arranged items so that children have little step-ups to get to the things in the house that they can use. One may find a step-up in the bathroom or near the sink. Some parents have arranged special low cupboards where children can get dishes to set the dinner table, or children may have their own small tables next to the large dining room table. Closets may have low hooks so that children may hang up their own clothes. Some parents have been able to set aside a special room in the house where children can play and get their toys from shelves accessible to them. This is a room where children cannot only work with colors and paints and look at books, but where a mother can come to discover with her children some of the meanings that natural things have for religious life.

In addition to this special room, the whole house is easily a place where children and parents can discover the meaning of the symbols of light and water and community. The family gathers around a table, the family members serve one another, eat together, and enjoy each other in this unity. Eating together is the perfect preparation for worshiping together; really "breaking bread" together in a Eucharistic service.

THE PARENT AS OBSERVER

If the Montessori teacher must be an observer of children, what about loving parents who watch their children from birth? Through daily living, parents should be skilled observers of their children's development. Parents then are the perfect teachers for their children, for parents are experienced in knowing what children want to understand and when to help them.

One mother described how she had planned to make a tree out of modeling clay to help her children understand their inner feelings for growth and upward movement. On the day when she was going to do this with her children it rained. The children went out to play and came home with mud on their shoes, knees, and hands. She decided that this would not be the appropriate time to discuss trees. Then one of them mentioned the fact that spring was coming and that there was a lot of water on the ground. In listening to her children talk about what they had discovered outdoors, she decided that, despite the muddiness, she would ask them to sit down at the kitchen table while she made something for them out of clay. After she began to make the tree and the children discovered what she was making, the mother sang a song about how Christ is like a tree. She said that tears came into her eyes because this was the first time she had shared with her children her own attitude toward Christ, and that she would not have believed such a thing possible. In fact, formerly she had been afraid to do anything like this with her children. Yet, her success convinced her that she could do this again, and could share more intimately with her children than she ever had before.

Through observation, this mother was able to discover many other things with her children. She listened to them talk to other children and to each other about the things that make up religious experience. Her children did not give definitions of the Trinity or even say that

God made the world. Rather, when they spoke at all about God, they were talking about a good time they had with their mother and father using the Christ candle, or breaking bread, or talking about water. The family sang songs before they ate and as they worked around the house. These songs said something about Christ as our Light and as the Good Shepherd who leads us to green pastures. The father did not preach to his children about God, but, rather, said just before meals: "Let us ask God to bless us and to help us to know what it is we should do. Let us remember those who are hungry and need food. Let us be grateful that Annie had such a good day at school today." These children developed a sense of the sacred because their parents were reverent toward each other, toward them, and toward the ordinary things of everyday life.

CONCLUSION

The home, then, is in every sense a church. It is a place where one can worship God through Christ and in the Spirit. We know that the church is the people of God in Christ. Within the home, are gathered the people of God. Parents should be aware that their homes can have a decor of silence. The colors used to decorate a home need not fight and make noise. The artistic representations in the home can be few and tasteful. Children can then look around from the day they open their eyes and see not only this tasteful decor, but a mother and father whose smiles tell them more than anything else what Christ looks like.

SUGGESTED READING

Article

Pohier, O. P., Jacques M. "Religious Mentality and Child Mentality," *Lumen Vitae Studies in Religious Psychology*, II, 1961. pp. 21–44.

4 Symbolism

In Chapter 3 we spoke of a good home relationship as one that gives children the opportunity to love and to know. We saw that a good first seven years makes it possible for children to know and love God. We talked about taking a longer look both at children and at the everyday, ordinary things around us. And finally, we spoke of the Montessori Method of teaching small children.

CONVENTIONAL AND NATURAL SYMBOLS

In this chapter, we would like to detail the ideas set forth in Chapter 3, and try to see how things in our everyday lives can speak to us of another reality beyond ourselves. When we look at things in this way, they become symbols. A symbol is something visible that expresses something invisible. There are two kinds of symbols: conventional and natural. A conventional symbol has a meaning because human beings have agreed to give it that meaning. A word is a conventional symbol. For example, the word "America" names a place we know about, our own country. The second kind of symbol, a natural symbol, is something we experience in everyday life, something in nature that we may hear, taste, touch, or smell and that expresses something deeper that cannot be sensed. A natural symbol does not require that we give it meaning. A natural symbol speaks for itself. Bread, for example, bespeaks life. Humans experience that they are alive, and want to stay alive. We see bread, something outside ourselves which, if eaten, keeps us alive. We reflect on experience: bread sustains life. Therefore, bread symbolizes life.

The importance of natural symbols is that they link our experience within to what is outside. Through these symbols we can know better what is going on inside ourselves. Natural symbols keep us from living in a dream world. They are a link between subjective and objective reality. We often hear that we must learn to see reality as it is. Natural symbols are a constant help toward this.

PREPARED ENVIRONMENT

Maria Montessori sensed the importance of natural symbols. This can be seen in the very arrangement of the prepared environment. The Montessori classroom gives the child what Maria Montessori called an "immersion in experience." This immersion provides the child with the possibility of seeing reality as it is. There are many natural symbols in a Montessori classroom—water, plants, fish, and other things of nature. In addition to natural symbols, there are objects—blocks, squares, and cylinders—which Montessori called "didactic apparatus." Though these objects are not, strictly speaking, natural symbols, they do present children with characteristics of real things. Montessori said that these objects help the children read everything that their environment and the world contain.

One of the Montessori exercises involves building the "brown stairs." This exercise uses ten rectangular prisms, each twenty centimeters long. Each prism increases in width and depth. The brown stairs can be built horizontally or vertically. The exercise helps the child to develop visual discrimination. Children who place the prisms one on top of the other seem to be filled with wonder. This experience of upwardness has some relationship to our experience of a tree.

Through this and similar exercises or happenings, humans experience growth and unity and see this reflected in nature. Thus, nature takes on a symbolic meaning. God, who is providence, uses natural symbols to convey a message to us. In this way natural symbols become religious symbols.

THE TREE SYMBOL

The ancients looked at a tree and saw it as something that was tall, straight, and upward-reaching. Yet it had roots in the ground. This tall, vertical shaft, the tree, seemed to be something that could connect humans with the divine. The tree also seemed to die and then come to life each year. It gave shade, protection, and fruit. The tree, then, became a symbol of life.

The tree is one of the earliest biblical images of life. In Genesis, we read of a paradise with a tree of the knowledge of good and evil, and a tree of life that could give immortality. These trees stood in the middle of the garden, the center of the universe, watered by the river spreading into four branches. Trees are mentioned often in the Old Testament, always bringing to mind the ideas of life, protection, and immortality. Prophets sat under trees. Saul and his companions sought shelter under a tree. In the wise sayings found in the Wisdom literature of the Bible, a tree is used to express the idea of life-giving wisdom. Finally, the prophets, especially Isaiah, spoke of the day when, "a shoot shall come from the stump of Jesse" (Isa. 11:1). This new shoot, a new tree from the family tree of David, was the Savior, Christ.

The time of the new tree of life came with the birth of Christ. The promise of life given to Abraham is fulfilled in Christ. From the tree of the cross, Christ entered into fullness of life. It was not until the apostles met the risen Christ that they realized that the tree of the cross made it possible for Jesus to pass over into a new life. Then they recalled what a tree meant to them and told us of the mystery of this life by using the imagery of the tree.

St. John gives us these words of Christ: "And I, when I am lifted up from the earth, will draw all . . . to myself." Later on, when St. John wrote to the Church of Ephesus, he said, "Let anyone who has an ear, listen to what the Spirit is saying to everyone who conquers, I will give permission to eat from the tree of life, that is in the paradise of God" (Rev. 2:7). It is Christ who speaks these words: "Everyone who conquers I will give permission to eat from the tree of life."

But how do we receive the fruit of the tree of life? It is by union with Christ that we receive it. And now we turn from the image of the tree to the image Christ used when he spoke of himself. Christ called himself a vine. He said, "I am the vine, you are the branches. Those who abide in me, and I in them, bear much fruit, because apart from me you can do nothing" (John 15:5). It is only when we are united to Christ as closely as branches to a vine that we can eat of the tree of life and live forever. Christ is the Source of our life.

CONCLUSION

We have just explained how natural symbols express the invisible. We spoke of the Montessori Method as an "immersion in experience." Finally, we talked about the meaning of the word tree in the Bible. Now we suggest that you make a tree for the children. However, before the children see this tree, they should already have played the game, "Here We Go 'Round the Mulberry Bush." No doubt they have climbed trees. Some of them know about or have tree houses. Most of them have certainly clung to their fathers' legs and played "Sally in the

Saucer." These ordinary actions of children show how all of us gather around someone who is the source of our life for us.

In the lesson, we suggest that the children be given the experience of watching a tree being painted. The children should be helped to notice that the roots are in the ground and yet the branches reach to the sky. In this way, they can begin to get an idea of the man Jesus, who is fully human, of the earth and fully divine. Let the children suggest activities related to trees, such as picking fruit, meeting and having a picnic under a tree, seeing how the birds nest in trees. These games lay the groundwork for a better knowledge of who Christ can be for them. Then when the tree is finished, sing about it. You need not tell the children, "Christ our Lord is like a tree." Instead, you may sing it. Singing this truth is a more subtle and effective means of presentation.

LESSONS

1. The Tree

General Objective:

To help the child begin to understand how a tree can remind us of Christ, the Source of our life.

For the Parent and the Teacher:

Aim: To see how a tree can remind us of the mysterious, unique union of Jesus with God (roots in ground, branches in the sky), of his mediatorship, of his redemptive life-giving love, of his union with all human beings. The growth of a tree is an image of the growth of a person. The individual's growth must resemble the upward thrust or growth of a tree that obeys an inner law and grows according to its own limitations and capabilities.

For the Lesson:

Aim: To help the children to understand through their knowledge of trees that trees can remind us of Christ, the source of our life. Remember that this is the first lesson. Do not try to bring out the point too strongly, because you are introducing children to symbols and trying to make them aware of their meaning. You are helping the children to identify consciously with symbols. Many adults find this difficult, so do not expect immediate success. You are laying the foundation for faith and a life of vision, and helping the children to see poetically, to see with wisdom.

Preparation: Pre-lessons with the children might include a picnic under a tree, playing "Here We Go 'Round the Mulberry Bush," "Sally in the Saucer," planting a small bush or tree, identifying different trees in a park, or gathering fruit from a tree.

Materials: Colored chalk or paints to paint a tree for the children, either on a large piece of paper, or on one the size that they use in class. If you prefer three-dimensional work (and it is most highly recommended), then use clay. For teachers with more experience in art media, torn tissue paper or paper and scissors may be used. The aim is to have the children experience something of the evolution or growth of a tree. This is why we are not suggesting that you use a picture of a tree already finished.

Conversation: Begin to paint, color, or model a tree, being sure to begin with the roots. Elicit from the children ideas of what they will soon see. When they notice roots, trunk, and branches help them to identify with the tree's efforts to reach the sky. Ask them what they do with a tree. Bring out answers that are concerned with the shade and protection a tree gives, its fruit, its use as a place to meet. Draw people dancing about a tree. This will illustrate both vertical and horizontal movement.

Activity: Sing a song about a tree. Hold hands for one verse. Make a gesture with open arms for another verse. These gestures symbolize the fact that we gather around Christ, the source of our life. The gesture of arms open and upward is one of surrender and one that is used at prayer.

Later, the children may paint trees or model them from clay. They may cut out pictures of trees, especially trees that have people under them. They may label trees. This latter activity prepares for the symbolism of the Christmas tree lesson.

With slides or films, you can repeat the lesson, emphasizing the same points. Remember that you cannot repeat enough, for you are laying a foundation for a second level of interpretation.

Use pictures of various trees. This time you can be more particular. Use some pictures of trees found in the Bible and explain them. For example, the cedars of Lebanon are large, majestic trees that live for centuries and are used in the Bible as symbols of power and greatness: "The trees of the lord are watered abundantly, the cedars of Lebanon, that he planted. In them the birds build their nests" (Ps. 104:16).

2. The Advent Wreath

General Objective:

To help the child prepare to celebrate the birthday of the King.

For the Parent and the Teacher:

Aim: To come to an understanding of the three comings of Christ: historical, sacramental, eschatological: Christ came in time; Christ comes and is present in the sacramental action of the church; Christ will come in glory at the final day when all is fulfilled. We prepare to celebrate these comings and thus recognize them by this deepened understanding.

For the Lesson:

Aim: To remind us that Christmas is a celebration of Christ's birthday by lighting candles.

Materials: A fir tree branch for each child. An old tin gelatin mold in which to arrange them. Candles and ribbons. A spoon for dirt if it is used. A candle extinguisher and a taper for lighting the candles.

Conversation: Give branches to all the children. Speak with them about the smell, color, feel of fir. Point out that the fir tree is an evergreen, that it is green even in winter. Help the children to realize the circular quality of the mold. Spoon dirt into the mold. Ask each child by name to come up and place a branch in the mold. Then insert the candles, tying bows on them if you wish, and talk about the meaning of light. (See Chapter 7.) Later the children can advance toward the light on the wreath from a distance and discover how they begin to see more as they approach the light. They also discover each other.

Activity: During this season each meeting of the children can include lighting of the wreath and singing an appropriate song.

3. The Christmas Tree

General Objective:

To celebrate the glory of the Lord Jesus.

For the Parent and the Teacher:

Aim: To lead the children to a realization of the beauty and glory of the risen Lord, whose beauty is made manifest by the deeds of His members.

Background: The Christmas tree custom is considered to be of pagan origin. Yet because of usage and our own realization of what a tree can mean, we can see that the glory of the church finds its source in Christ, and its visible manifestation in its members.

For the Lesson:

Aim: To decorate a tree that reminds us of Christ the source of our life.

Materials: Ornaments made by the children.

Conversation: Sit in a circle around a small covered object, a pine tree (If possible, a potted one to be planted by the class after Christmas). Each child has a small box with an ornament he or she has made. The teacher unveils the tree. The children talk about it, about watering it, playing around it, and so forth. (Preparation for concept of an evergreen has been made in the Advent wreath lesson.) Then have the children tell why they made the ornaments. (To show their love for Jesus by decorating a tree that reminds them of him. As children make the decorations they can be told simply, "We are making some beautiful things for our Christmas tree.") Unveil the tree. (A covered object focuses attention through curiosity.) Then call on each child to place an ornament on the tree. If the tree has lights, darken the room and light them after the ornaments have been placed on the tree to show how light enhances our gift, our work.

Activity: After the children have presented the gift of their ornaments, sing a Christmas carol or another song.

SUGGESTED READINGS

Books

Campbell, Joseph. *Myths to Live By.* New York: Bantam Books, 1988. (See especially Chapters 1 and 2.)

Eliade, M. and Kitagawa, J. M. *The History of Religions.* Chicago: University of Chicago Press, 1959.

Jung, Carl J. *Man and His Symbols.* New York: Doubleday, 1964. (See especially Part One.)

Silverstein, Shel. *The Giving Tree.* New York: Harper and Row, 1964.

Vann, Gerald, O. P. *The Paradise Tree.* New York: Sheed and Ward, 1959. (See especially Chapter 1.)

5 Cosmic, Psychological, and Social Symbols

In Chapter 4 we discussed symbols and how they help us to understand the invisible. We pointed out that the Montessori Method gives the child a possibility for learning through experience. We considered the biblical image of a tree, and suggested some lessons that could be formed around the notion of a tree, an Advent wreath, or a Christmas tree. Finally, we suggested that the children sing about the tree, about life, and especially about Christ, who is the source of our life.

LEVELS OF SYMBOLISM

There were three levels of symbolism in the tree lesson: cosmic, psychological, and social. The cosmic level was the symbol "tree" that related the children to something in creation. The psychological level was the experience the children had watching someone "make" a tree. The children can now relate this experience to other experiences they have of trees: for example, tree houses, mulberry trees, and so forth. The third level was the social one. The children grouped together and sang about the tree. In this way they were given an opportunity to relate socially to others.

We speak about these three levels of symbolism—cosmic, psychological, and social—in order to better understand how humans develop their system of symbols. Each person has different experiences and these experiences help to understand life. For example, a person who cannot eat all foods has a peculiar understanding of eating. When that person comes to the table mannerisms and attitudes are conditioned by the inability to eat particular foods. Eating, for this person, could very well be most unpleasant.

Development of the Symbol System

Why are we concerned about these levels of symbolism? If, from personal experience, each individual develops a particular symbol system, it is important that we give children experiences that will help them to understand life. The things of the world and the actions of everyday life are saying, or, symbolizing something to children. If parents help them to understand this and to relate to it properly, they will help their children in approaching all of life.

But this ability to communicate the meaning of life to children through symbols requires of adults a sensitivity, an ability to communicate to children their own understanding of life and of the experiences of life.

The Teacher's Attitude

The teacher, and more especially, the parent, is the link between the child and the truth discovered through experience. Often, as mentioned earlier, when one visits a Montessori classroom, it is difficult to find the teacher who is usually not in front of the children but alongside them. The teacher, then, does not have to know all the answers, but must constantly maintain a certain degree of humility. Arthur Jersild has written in his book, *When Teachers Face Themselves*, that humility is shown in the person of one who is able to wait and to be silent. That person can wait, not expecting to immediately understand each question from within or have a response to each query from without; not expecting to reach an instantaneous insight or to have an instantaneous answer; not feeling guilty when assailed by doubts about something believed to be a certainty. These words are consoling when one thinks of the role of the parent as a teacher and communicator to the child of religious experience. It is not necessary for the parent to be a brilliant theologian. But it is necessary that the parent be able to stay at a child's side, humbly and respectfully trying to understand the mystery of God's love for each person.

This attitude of waiting, of humility before the mystery of religion, makes the teacher-parent a communicator with three qualities that Montessori stressed. She spoke first of the teacher as an "observer." Montessori often repeated the dictum, "Observation is a form of pedagogy." This fits the role of loving parents who watch their child's every move—the child's first smile, first look of recognition, first words. In order to know what to say to a child one must learn to listen to what the child is saying. Montessori said the teacher must have an almost scientific interest in every "free natural manifestation of the child." "Our one duty," she wrote, "is to learn from him on the spot, and to serve him, as best we can." This ability of keen observation made her decide to allow the children to learn while sitting, or even sprawled out, on the floor. She noticed that children instinctively assumed positions that would best enable them to learn according to their own physical development.

Second, Montessori said that the teacher must be the "exemplar." Enough has been written about the necessity of good example. However, Montessori asked the teacher to be an example in such a way as to be one with the child in everything the child does. Nothing was asked of the child that the teacher did not do first. It is not the teacher's voice alone but every act, that calls to the child. All adults have seen children mimicking the things their parents do.

Third, Montessori talked about the teacher as "programmer." If teachers or parents observe well and are careful to reflect all that the children do, then they will be able to plan properly how best to communicate to the children what it is they should discover. When we are thinking in terms of religion, more is required. An existential experience of Christ and of God the Creator, an understanding of the Bible, and a reflective attitude are necessary. This is precisely why this book presents background material for the various symbols. If parents know the material and reflect on it, they will be able to communicate it when the proper moment arrives. We are speaking of an ability to associate what we see—trees, rocks, water—with their deepest meaning, a meaning we know and have reflected upon. We do not, therefore, "program" truths or lessons. But we know what we would like our children to know and we can communicate it when they are ready.

THE SYMBOLISM OF WATER

With this in mind let us think together about what water can mean to us and to our relationship with God. For ancient man, water was a source of life and death. It is not unusual then to read the opening verses of Genesis and learn about the creation of the world in terms of the Spirit of God brooding over waters and bringing forth life. When the Israelites escaped the slavery of the Egyptians they did so by passing through the waters of the Red Sea. When they lived in the desert, they were constantly aware of their need for water. It came to symbolize for them the gift of life. In one of their thanksgiving songs they sang:

"Tremble, O earth, at the presence of the LORD,
   at the presence of the God of Jacob,

Cosmic, Psychological, and Social Symbols   **29**

who turns the rock into a pool of water,
The flint into a spring of water" (Ps. 114:7–8).

The New Testament writers, because of their experience of Christ and their profound understanding of the Old Testament, were keenly aware of water as the source of life. St. John, for example, described the Hebrew harvest feast, a time when the Jews recalled the Lord's help in the past. God had given them water and brought them through water to a fruitful land of milk and honey. They sang and waved palm branches and begged for the gift of autumn rain. At the high point of this feast, on the last day, the Jews carried in solemn procession a golden jug of water. St. John writes, "On the last day of the festival, the great day, while Jesus was standing there, he cried out, 'Let anyone who is thirsty come to me, and let the one who believes in me drink'" (John 7:37). All these experiences of thirst, and of salvation through water, were preparing God's people to understand that eternal life comes from Christ, the source of living water.

In order for children to understand how Christ is this to all of us, it is important that we talk with them about ordinary water. We have not spoken about all the other good experiences of water that children can have to help them appreciate this symbol. How many times does the excitement of a thunderstorm, the refreshment of rain, the power of waves beating on a beach remind us of the presence of the holy? It is to be hoped that such experiences will someday help the children to truly hear such words of Christ as, "Put out into the deep . . . " (Luke 5:4); "I am thirsty" (John 19:28); ". . . those who drink of the water that I will give them will never be thirsty. The water that I will give will become in them a spring of water gushing up to eternal life." (John 4:14).

CONCLUSION

In this section we have spoken about the three levels of symbolism: cosmic, psychological, and social. We have seen how each person comes to a particular understanding of life, and the symbolic meaning of the things of life. We know how important it is then to help in this process by providing the possibilities for a true understanding of life. We spoke about the teacher or parent who is, above all, a communicator—an observer, an exemplar, and a programmer. Finally we talked about the symbolism of water and how its deepest meaning comes from Christ's words about water; that the eternal life we receive from Christ is like living water.

1. Water

General Objective:

To help the children to understand how water can remind them of Christ who satisfies our thirst.

For the Parent and the Teacher:

Aim: To understand all the potentialities of water: powerful, death-and life-giving, cleansing, refreshing, healing, nourishing, unifying.

Background: Christ is the dew that came down to water the earth and give life. The image of abundant and life-giving water is used throughout the Old Testament to signify the gifts of God and the blessings that will ensue when the Messiah comes. Christ spoke of himself in these terms when he said, "Let anyone who is thirsty come to me" (John 7:37).

For the Lesson:

Aim: To understand how Christ refreshes us.

Materials: A mat, a plant in dry soil. A pitcher of water.

Conversation: Invite the children to sit in a circle. Ask a child to place a mat in the center. Bring out a plant that is dry and cultivated so that the plant may be taken out and the roots exposed. Pass the plant around. Ask, "What does this plant need?" "Why?" Ask them to repeat after you, "Lord, send my roots rain." (This is the last line of Gerard Manley Hopkins's poem, "Justus Quidem tu es, Domine." In this sonnet, the poet asks the Lord why all he does ends in disappointment, while others prosper. He notes that banks are covered with leaves, birds build nests, and he does not "breed one work that wakes." It ends, "Mine, O thou Lord of life, send my roots rain.")

After the children have examined the plant and seen how plants drink in water, ask one child to water it. Then bring out a veiled pitcher of water and unveil it. Very slowly pour water into glasses. Let the children watch it cascade into the glasses. Then, with a beautiful gesture of service, pass a glass of water and a napkin to each child.

Activity: Drink the water together and sing or recite Psalm 23. Then, talk about how good this water is.

Cosmic, Psychological, and Social Symbols

SLIDES, FILMS, AND VIDEOS

Films about water are an excellent means of understanding the idea that life comes from water. An ordinary collection of slides showing water scenes or activities of people with water can open up more discussion on the properties of water mentioned above.

6 Principles of Teaching

In the last chapter we discussed the levels of symbolism that condition a child to build attitudes toward life. We said that there were three levels of symbolism: the cosmic (things of nature such as water), the psychological (both the encounter with the symbol and the importance of a proper happy experience of it), and the social aspect (the relation of the child's experience to other children). All these and similar experiences make up one's understanding of life. The way the parent or teacher provides for such a meeting with ordinary things helps the child toward acquiring a rich understanding of life. We may say that they help the child to see, hear, and touch and thereby to begin to form a conceptual background. The parent or teacher is really helping the child to "build a language" that will best express an understanding of life. We have the choice of helping a child to build a true language with words that best express understanding, or of helping the child spin fantasies and to live in a dream world.

The lesson on water followed a certain pattern or form. In this chapter we will present the principles underlying this pattern. Then, there will be a presentation of the symbol of the rock.

METHOD OF TEACHING

It is necessary for us to understand the activity of children as they are working. Maria Montessori said that a child works with a certain rhythm and that this rhythm enables the child to begin again with new energy each time. She called this rhythm the "cycle of activity." She simply watched a child select some work, continue working with it until satisfied, and then put it away. To every cycle of activity there is a beginning, a middle, and an end. This is not new. Aristotle spoke in a similar way about the elements of a good drama. The difference between little Johnny's or Sally's activity and Aristotle's concept of action is that Johnny and Sally do not work toward a particular goal. They do not clean a table to get it clean or sweep a floor to get rid of the dust. They work because they have within them the desire to begin, to continue, and to end, and not because they want to get something done. For this reason they are not in a hurry. This is why they can finish building a tower, knock it down, and then start all over again.

This may seem impractical to us, but Johnny and Sally are satisfying a law within themselves—laying down a pattern of activity. Do we not do the same thing when we play or dance? A dance begins, continues, ends. It does not go anywhere. It merely expresses a rhythm within us and so satisfies our desire for order. This is true of a good poem, of a piece of music, or of the beat of a wave on the beach.

In working with children we must respect this inner order. Montessori said, "The cycle must have been completed. So whatever intelligent activity we chance to witness in a child—even if it seems absurd to us, or contrary to our wishes (provided, of course, that it does him no harm) we must not interfere, for the child must always be able to finish the cycle of activity on that his heart is set."

A little girl in a grocery store walked along a counter ledge. Her mother wanted to finish shopping so she could leave the store. She called to the child and told her to step down from the ledge and come along. The little girl replied, "Wait! I'm not finished." Finished doing what? She had not finished the effort she had begun. Other applications of this principle might prove helpful in dealing with your own child. For example, Johnny will not put his toys away if he is not allowed to finish some other, perhaps, useless activity, such as walking along a crack in the sidewalk.

ORDER OF PRESENTING A LESSON

This principle also applies to the presentation of a lesson, or to our method of teaching. In a Montessori classroom and in your own home, lessons are most successful when given to an individual child. This is called working one-to-one. An effective lesson with a group of children usually comes later. For the most part there is no social life to speak of for three- and four-year-olds. The child learns first to live with himself or herself, and only later to relate to others. This applies perfectly to the home situation where learning is not formal but, rather, incidental. However, the lessons in this book may be presented either to an individual child or to a group of children.

The first part of a lesson is called the initiation. The teacher must first arouse the attention of the child or children—if possible, ask consent to begin. In order not to force children to do something before they are ready, we ask them whether they wish to stay or to go away. This gives the child another chance for development toward maturity—free conscious choice. Asking a child whether he or she wishes to participate in a certain activity assures the teacher of the second point: choosing the right moment. The teacher must also be reasonably sure of the child's success. This is another way of stating the old adage, "Nothing succeeds like success." The teacher should then begin to speak intimately to the child. She must look at the child. This is something special for each individual child. Finally, to ensure success in giving the lesson the teacher must divert the attention of the child from everything but the object of the lesson.

The second part of the lesson is the presentation. For small children this consists of demonstration rather than wordy description. Description should be avoided because, even a young child has learned to tune you out. The child is learning to speak and if you speak a lot will miss what you are illustrating. The first step is to demonstrate exactly, using a few words simply and truthfully. Then, just as you must divert the child's attention, so must you isolate the object about which you are speaking. If you wish to speak of a tree, do not put birds in it or animals under it. Establish the idea of a tree, first. Often, for example, a child may be taught the color red by being shown a picture of an apple with other fruit around it. Already you have a clutter of ideas: fruit, food, store, money, mother, kitchen—everything but the color red.

The last part of the lesson, and probably the most important part, we call continuation. First, the teacher allows the child to repeat. If, however, the child persists in using the materials incorrectly, the teacher helps the child put them away. There is nothing to be learned through the repetition of error. Do not give the children the "illusion" that they know something. This is playing false to children and they soon will learn to distrust you. But rather than point out errors, the teacher should emphasize what the child is doing correctly. Then, observing the child the teacher learns to lead the child to progressive interest and perfection. Often a child will say with a glint in the eye, "Now you're going to make it harder," enjoying the challenge. Finally, the teacher directs the child to put away the work when it is finished. This encourages the child to do what is natural, to complete what has been begun.

THE SYMBOLISM OF THE ROCK

Having considered the technique of the lesson, we will now consider a third biblical image: the rock. Ancient humans looked at solid crags, unchanging boulders, and precious stones, and became fascinated with them. A rock meant protection, strength, even the dwelling place of a god. To the ancient civilizations of the Old Testament, a rock represented solidity, unchangeableness, and the faithfulness of their God. Their God never changed, never retracted promises. To them this was fidelity. A rock was the symbol of faithfulness. In a song that became a kind of catechism for Judaism at the time of Christ the Hebrews sang:

> The Rock, his work is perfect
> and all his ways are just.
> A faithful God, without deceit,
> just and upright is he (Deut. 32:4).

The Hebrews acknowledged this firmness of God's word by saying "Amen." The word "Amen" comes from a root meaning "to be trustworthy." Even today, "Amen" is used to say "Yes," to signify agreement. In worship the leader recites a prayer. All the people show their agreement to this prayer by saying "Amen."

In the New Testament we find that the early Christians showed their belief in Christ by using the word "Amen." The early Christians realized that Christ was the Promised One who proved God's faithfulness. St. John gives Christ the name "Amen." He writes, "The words of the Amen, the faithful and true witness, origin of God's creation" (Rev. 3:14). This beginning of God's creation is Christ, our faithful and true witness on whom our whole faith rests.

During the celebration of the Eucharist, the church asks us to say "Amen" to the action of the celebrant so that his action may be our action. We say "Amen" when the priest raises the bread and the cup together and says, "Through him, with him, in him, in the unity of the Holy Spirit, all glory and honor is yours, almighty Father, for ever and ever. Amen!" We say, "Yes, this is so."

How will we teach these things to children? Remember, they do not need to know all this. Instead we will talk about a rock and sing "Amen." From this beginning, we will proceed to lay down an understanding of how solid Christ is in whom we believe, how true he is, how grateful we are to be able to put our faith and trust in him. Finally, at every Eucharist, we will renew together our belief in him.

There was once a boy who sensed something special about rocks, and iron and metal pieces. He lived in a place called Sarcenat, a tiny mountain village in France. "I was certainly no more than six or seven," he recalled some time later, "when I began to feel drawn by matter—more exactly by something that 'shone' at the heart of matter." The boy secretly hoarded commonplace metallic objects: a plow key, nails, spent cartridge shells. "I withdrew into the contemplation of my 'God of Iron.' Why iron? Because in my childish experience nothing was harder, tougher, more durable. Stability: that undoubtedly has been for me the fundamental attribute of Being."

Finally, one day he found that the iron piece was rusted. Despair overwhelmed him. To console himself, he searched for more durable idols. The region around Sarcenat abounds in volcanic craters, and he dug up bits of quartz, amethyst, and chalcedony. His entire spiritual life as he looked back on it, seemed to him merely a development of that boyhood vision. This boy grew up to be Teilhard de Chardin, the great Jesuit philosopher and paleontologist, who perceived in a unique way the unity of God and the world.

CONCLUSION

We have not yet spoken of such things as rock collecting, rock-climbing, and playing "King of the Mountain." Watch children's fascination with rocks. What will you say to them? What awareness will you have? Can we not prepare children to hear such words as, "You are Peter, and on this rock I will build my church" (Matt. 16:18), or hear Peter's words to the early Christians, "Come to him, a living stone, though rejected by mortals but chosen and precious in God's sight, and like living stones, let your souls be built into a spiritual house, to be a holy priesthood, to offer spiritual sacrifices acceptable to God through Jesus Christ" (1 Pet. 2:4, 5).

LESSON

Rock

General Objective:

To help the children understand that God's fidelity is rock—like by presenting a rock to them.

For the Parent and the Teacher:

Aim: To know what the word "Amen" means to the Christian, and to understand God's faithfulness to us. Try to study rock formations, chemical reactions on rocks, the properties of protectiveness of rocks, stability found in rocks.

For the Lesson:

Aim: To consider rocks and learn what it is to be faithful.

Materials: A large beautiful rock, a mat to slide it on, a pan and some water. Smaller gems to look at now or later.

Conversation: Cover a large, heavy rock with a veil. It should be of colored marble or quartz. Invite the children to sit in a circle. Ask them individually if they wish to stay or go away. This gives the child the chance to make a choice and be faithful to it. If one child says he will stay, and then becomes fidgety and anxious to leave, remind him of the choice he made at the beginning. If another wishes to go away and then comes to see what is going on, remind her of her choice to stay away. This is an exercise for the child in free conscious choice and a preparation for really saying "Amen" to a commitment to the Lord and to all brothers and sisters.

After the rock is unveiled, slide it along the mat from one child to another. The children may want to lift it. Let them do so. You may emphasize the quality of strength that a rock implies. Small rocks may be passed back and forth at the same time and you may explain that these were chipped off larger ones. Talk about the rock, name it, put it in a pan of water to see if it will dissolve or change. Tell the children that rocks do not change; that they will be able to watch this one every day to see if it does change. This emphasizes the most important point—that a rock shows the constancy of God, our rock.

Activity: When the lesson is over, sing a song about a rock. Go for a "walk" with the rock and put it in a special place in the room. This is a gesture symbolic of the whole Christian life—a journey.

SLIDES, FILMS, AND VIDEOS

Collect slides or get a short concept video tape on rocks to show to the children. Discuss again the properties of rock. This time you should be able to discuss such passages as "Be to me a rock of refuge" (Ps. 70:3); "Shade of a great rock in weary land" (Isa. 32:2); "Laid the foundation on rock" (Luke 6:48). (See also Psalms 17, 18, 30, 91, 94; Deut. 32:3, 4; Rom. 9:33; 1 Cor. 10:4.)

DIMENSIONAL ILLUSTRATION

Place a small wooden house on a rock in a pan, and another on a mound of sand in a pan. Ask one child to pour water from a sprinkling can onto the house and to imagine that it is rain falling on the house. Notice what happens to the house placed on the sand. Tell the children that this is a story that our Lord told to show us how God must be our rock.

BOOKS AND PICTURES

Children should have the opportunity to look through some of the many good books on rock formation. These scientific books do not destroy the symbolism of the rock, but provide the children with correct notions of rocks, lava, and so forth, in order to come to a better understanding of the earth. To classify rocks and collect them without reference to God will still be a religious activity, since to understand God we must understand the works of God's hand.

SUGGESTED READINGS

Books

Bond, Gladys Baker. *The Magic Friend–Maker.* Racine, Wisconsin: Whitman Publishing Co. 1966. (This is a story for children, too.)
Danielou, Jean. *God and the Ways of Knowing.* New York: Meridian Books, 1962. (See especially Chapter 1.)
Gelin, Albert. *The Key Concepts of the Old Testament.* New York: Sheed and Ward, 1955.
Lindbergh, Anne Morrow. *A Gift From the Sea.* New York: Vintage, 1955. (See especially Chapter 6.)
Montessori, Maria. *The Absorbent Mind.* India: The Theosophical Publishing House, 1961. (See especially Chapter 15.)
——— , *Montessori Method.* New York: Schocken, 1964. (See especially Chapter 6.)
Rambusch, Nancy McCormick. *Learning How to Learn.* Baltimore, Md.: Helicon, 1963. (See especially Chapter 2.)

Article

Kobler, John. "The Priest Who Haunts the Catholic World," *Saturday Evening Post* (October 12, 1963), pp. 43–51.

7 Discipline and Silence

In Chapter 6 we suggested that the children learn an "Amen" song. We linked the saying or singing of "Amen" to an experience of rock. Perhaps all of the Christian life may be summed up in this simple experience. Every follower of Christ must learn to say, as Christ said, "Yes, be it so." The Blessed Virgin Mary, the great image of the church, helped bring about our salvation through a constant, faithful, "Yes, be it done to me." At the high point during the Eucharist when the totality of revelation is expressed, all present join themselves to the offering of Christ to his Father with a great "Amen."

In the lesson on rock, we tried to carry out the techniques of a lesson that we outlined at the beginning of Chapter 6. In the first part, the initiation, we suggested that you arouse the interest of the children by presenting to them something covered with a piece of cloth. Children are curious to see what is under the cloth. We are appealing to their sense of mystery. The cloth also helps you to speak intimately to the children and it diverts their attention from other things in the room. During the presentation part of the lesson, the rock was carefully unveiled, examined with very few words and passed around to each child. Finally, in order to continue the lesson properly we suggested that you help the children discuss the properties of rock. Sometimes it may be helpful to repeat their comments in order to lead them into a deeper understanding. We indicated that after an "Amen" song you should go for a walk with the rock and place it in a special place in the room. This is not merely a device to get the rock put away. There we initiated a gesture which is symbolic of the Christian's whole life. We can call it "Journeying."

Every person joins with a community of pilgrims—moving forward toward transcendant spiritual life, life with God. It is important for a man to feel this in a solemn way. The questions of each age are, "Where am I going? Where did I come from? Who am I?" God our

Father in his love for us revealed to us our destinies. God gave us his Son to show us the way, the truth, to be our light. God gave us the Spirit to keep this pursuit alive.

DISCIPLINE

In this chapter we want to discuss something underlying all principles of education and that is the notion of discipline. We have said that, for the most part, lessons in the Montessori classroom are given one-to-one. Children must first learn that they are persons and only then can they discover how to relate socially to others. Certainly, what every person must learn in order to relate properly to the world is discipline. One definition of discipline is "active self-control and willed obedience through 'conquest of liberty' developing responsibility for self-regulation of behavior." (Rambusch, et al, op. cit.)

How do we help a child to achieve self-discipline? Montessori says a command will not order the complex psychomuscular system of a person into a path of evolution. Self–discipline is not something imposed from without, but something that comes from within. A child must someday come to the realization that, "I tell my hand to do this and it does it." Montessori said that discipline or obedience can be secured only through a complex formation of the mental personality; in order to obey we must have not only the desire to obey, but also the ability to obey.

In order to understand how a child may come to this type of self–regulation of behavior, let us look at its opposite, what Montessori called "deviated" behavior or the "deviated child."

THE DEVIATED CHILD

The deviated child is a Montessori term denoting a child who lacks an integration of mind and body (this is not a term we would use today, but it expressed a valid concept). One can see this first in the child's disorderly movements. What is involved is not that the child runs around aimlessly or destructively, but that there is a lack of ability to direct hands and feet in a coordinated manner. The way a child walks, the way he or she handles the self, and other things, tell us whether inner discipline has been achieved. A second symptom of a deviated child is that there is too much fantasy in his or her work. We are all familiar with the imaginative playmate or the whopper tale stage that a child goes through. This is normal. What Montessori observed as deviation is excessive withdrawal from reality, inability to see and cope with things as they are, and constant chatter about schemes and things that are not possible. Third, the deviated child has more of a tendency to imitate than other children have. We notice this when a child always does what others do, or even when a child is "too good." The child who over-scrupulously carries out the instructions of a teacher is still undisciplined. Not regulating personal behavior, the child becomes the automaton of the teacher or of the group leader.

There are many more signs of the undisciplined or deviated child. These are all familiar. What we should like to warn against is labeling the independent child, the one who is assertive, as undisciplined. This child has perhaps the best possibility of achieving inner discipline.

Since the ability to obey comes from within, the parent or teacher must help the deviated child by feeding the child's intellect, body, and emotions. Often a child misbehaves because ability to think is not challenged. The child is bored. We all know the feeling of power and strength that comes from a stimulating conversation, from exposure to ideas. The young child is most sensitive to images. The child wishes to produce. Lack of stimulation causes restlessness. "Mother, what can I do?" the child asks. The child should be given not only colors to match, or forms to build, but even be allowed to help bake a cake if this feeds the intellect.

All of us are familiar with our own undisciplined behavior when we are hungry. The cure is obvious. But what about muscular activity? This, too, feeds the body. There is much talk today about the child who does not creep or crawl enough because of being placed too often in a playpen. Current research shows that it is through creeping and crawling that a child organizes the functions of the spinal cord and the proper function of the brain. Montessori noticed that children love to scale fences and reasoned that this effort at balancing was necessary to bodily organization. Hence, she painted a line on a floor and encouraged a "walking-the-line" game. According to Getman and Kane in *The Physiology of Readiness*, such practice in coordination, balance, eye-level coordination, eye movements, form-recognition, and visual memory makes the entire body a supporting and contributing action system for the interpretation and comprehension of the symbols of the classroom.

We are familiar with the behavior that stems from hunger, but are we aware of the insecurity and anxiety that comes from starved emotions? Are children not hyperactive because the are searching frantically for some assurance of love? We must look for ways to assure children that they are accepted. We must help them to accept and love themselves. This is called "feeding the emotions."

Victorian and puritanical backgrounds, coupled with an American fixation on cleanliness, have helped us neglect an important factor in

Nurturing Your Child's Spirit

feeding the emotions, namely, communication through touch. Dr. Smiley Blanton asked his male patients, "How long has it been since you've taken a walk with your arm around your wife? Do you ever get down on the living room floor and roughhouse the children? Has your family ever tried holding hands around the dinner table when you say grace?" From such communication, children can gain the inner strength to organize behavior. Since the skin is the largest organ of communication we have, perhaps it would be well to allow more water, sand, and mud play so that children have greater contact with the world through touch. Moreover, we know that Montessori encouraged learning shapes and geometric figures through touch. Children learn what a circle is not only by looking at it but by tracing the contours with the tips of their fingers.

ESTABLISHMENT OF DISCIPLINE

But how do we practically help a child to self-discipline: by giving the child what Montessori called "liberty within limits." What are the limits? The good of all. In order for some children to understand what is necessary for the good of all, they must occasionally be isolated from other children. This should not be done in a punishing way, but, rather, by gently removing the child from the rest of the group and allowing her or him to watch the others. This does not mean putting the child in the corner, facing the wall. The child must be allowed and even asked to watch the rest. Another way to handle an emotionally neglected child is to keep the child with you. How many times does Johnny act up because he wants you to pay attention to him? Is he not saying, in a rather annoying way, "Pay attention to me?" Another effective means toward treating this problem is to let another child do the correcting. It is sometimes easier for a child to accept correction from someone her own age. Dr. Jane Nelson and her colleagues have expanded these suggestions in many books notably, *Positive Discipline*.

In order to give the child a chance to make a free choice, even when we want her to stop what she is doing, we should offer two alternatives instead of one. That is, instead of saying, "Stop this and do that," we may say, "You cannot do this because it is dangerous. You may do this or that." This not only takes the edge off the prohibition, but it gives the child a chance to make a choice.

Finally, to discourage teachers from nagging, Montessori told them not to correct a child immediately everytime he or she gets to push in a chair, roll a rug properly, or perform any other action that keeps the room in order. She suggested that the teacher wait until a time when the children are gathered together for a group lesson and then make a game out of pushing in a chair or rolling a rug. This prevents embarrassment to the one child who forgets, and facilitates learning in a positive way. Educators speak today about "the wrong form of reinforcement." They say that a "No, don't do that," may trigger off a more firm desire to do it. It is, then, much more effective to play a game about what should be done. This positive means is not unknown to an adult world that uses humor and satire to effect change. A small gesture of complimenting the positive things children do and thus helping them to see for themselves the less polished areas of their work is another way of correction.

GROUND RULES

Finally, in a Montessori classroom there are certain ground rules that, if kept consistently, bring about this liberty within limits. They are: 1. Children must keep their hands off one another's work unless invited. 2. Children must put away work before beginning another task. 3. Arrange the room so that these two rules are facilitated. Shelves should be at a proper level. The work should be properly spaced on the shelves, and there should be no toy box in which everything is "dumped." Chaos breeds chaos. 4. Children must wait their turn. This last rule is a part of what Montessori calls "inhibitory exercises." Self–discipline is learning to tell oneself when to do something. Often this involves waiting. Since a Montessori teacher and most parents cannot attend to everything at once, a child is often asked to wait. A pat on the head is a way of saying through touch, rather than through many words, that we are too busy to help. If they know they are accepted, children can wait. They will tell themselves to wait. This is the beginning of self–discipline.

THE SILENCE GAME

The high point in the Montessori Method is achieved when a child can successfully participate in what Montessori called the "Silence Game." Some mothers, acquainted with the Montessori Method, in a great moment of disorder in their homes, have asked the children to play the Silence Game. It proves to be a restorer of order, a moment of reflection, an opportunity to gather oneself together and begin again. Dr. Maria Harris has written a book about the seven steps of women's spirituality. *Dance of the Spirit* gives the adult woman experiences for herself of what she may only begin to nurture in children.

There are four principles behind the Silence Game. First, silence, and the Silence Game should never be used at the beginning of the school year. It must be led up to as the children gain in muscular control and awareness of the collective interests of the group. There are remote preparations for the Silence Game. Games such as walking on a line, songs which require actions and gestures, any activity which challenges the body, or that demands listening and observation is a preparation for the discipline of silence. Second, the Silence Game involves the control of more than the speech mechanism. Voluntary silence means that the child wills to cease all activity. Forcing the child to keep the tongue still is not silence. The child's wiggling body may be "screaming." Third, the prepared environment, the colors of the room, for example, should foster silence. Just as speech is learned in an environment rich in language, so must silence be learned in a muted environment. Fourth, when the child achieves the self-mastery of silence, he or she has become aware of another deeper dimension of the self.

Briefly, in the Silence Game the children group around the teacher in a semi-dark room. They are invited to gradually relax themselves: relax feet, knees—let go muscularly. They go limp; heads go back, mouths slacken, eyes droop; they are completely quiet. Then the teacher goes quietly to the door and whispers the name of each child in turn. The child tiptoes to the door and stands quietly at the side of the teacher. Then they go back to their places very quietly in a group. The time may be lengthened by asking the children to return to their places one by one. The point of the game is that silence comes from listening and in this case the children are listening for their names.

The game may be summarized in this way: 1. Darken the room. 2. Listen. 3. Respond. The response period of the game may take many forms. Once there is silence in the room, the parent or teacher may read a passage of Scripture to the children. Or, the child may be called individually and the verse of a psalm can be spoken softly to them. The pattern of call and response is an ancient one. It is used in the Old Testament, as in God calling to Moses.

The lesson on light will include the beginning of the Silence Game. We will darken the room and light a candle. Later, we will call the children one by one.

The Symbolism of Light

Ancient men and women saw fire, or light, as a source of good and evil. In order to insure that it would be a source of good, they had fire festivals in honor of the gods. Fire soon became a way for them to communicate with the gods. Choice pieces of a sacrificial victim were burned in a sacred fire and the people saw in the rising smoke a way to contact the gods.

In the Old Testament, fire was usually part of the manifestation of God to the people. Since the Hebrews thought of their God as one who acts, the ever–burning, active fire that both purified and destroyed was a sign of the presence of the Lord. God, from a burning bush, called to Moses and told him of his presence (Ex. 3:2, 3). When the Israelites were lost in the desert, a pillar of fire guided them through the night (Ex. 13:21). Moses received the law on Mount Sinai and the whole mountain was "wrapped in smoke, because the LORD descended upon it in fire" (Ex. 19:18).

In somewhat the same way as ancient religious tribes, the Israelites used fire in their worship. The holocaust was the sacrifice in which the entire animal was consumed in the fire on the altar. Fire was a transforming element by which the victim became God's possession.

These ideas of fire as a sign of the presence of God, as a light that leads the way through the darkness, and as an element that purifies and makes holy that which it touches, were all present to the minds of the New Testament writers who wrote about their experience of Christ. St. Luke records Christ's words, "I came to bring fire to the earth, and how I wish it were already kindled" (Luke 12:49). Christ was speaking of what his coming meant. Christ came to die and pass over to the Father. Through Christ's death and resurrection we are transformed by the purifying fire that Christ was to kindle. The tongues of fire on Pentecost showed the presence of the Lord in the Spirit who was poured forth on all. Pentecost was now the day of the New Law written on human hearts (Acts 2:1).

Finally, St. John speaks not so much about fire but about evil as darkness and good as light. He records Christ's words, "I am the light of the world. Whoever follows me will never walk in darkness, but will have the light of life" (John 8:12). Today, in our Easter Service, we have the lighting of the new fire, reminding us of Christ's meaning for us. The Paschal Candle stands for Christ and light, and is likened to the pillar of fire that led the Israelites by night out of Egypt, the land of darkness.

CONCLUSION

In the lesson on light we are suggesting that you help your child see the possibility to understand Christ as the light who shows us the way as we journey. All this is experienced magnificently in our Easter Service when all the people light their candles from the great candle that represents Christ. The candles on the altar and the candles on your table at home can say the same thing to children. What speaks to them when they experience the candles on a Christmas tree, or a camp fire, or the sun rising over a lake?

Light

General Objective:

To help the child experience the need for Christ, our light, by lighting a candle in a darkened room.

For the Parent and the Teacher:

Aim: To understand all the properties of light and fire: it purifies, transforms, consumes, brings warmth, illuminates, and preserves. Light helps us to see one another. The closer we are to the light, the more we can see. Borrowing light from one candle to give it to another does not diminish the first candle. Notice the intimacy that is created by the lighting of a candle in the midst of a group that is in semidarkness.

Background: Read over the light service for Easter, especially the Exsultet. Notice the use of the word "light" in the Bible. For example, "Darkness covered the face of the deep . . . then God said 'Let there be light'." (Gen. 1:2–3). See also the Psalms 26, 36, 49, 138. Read over the Gospel of St. John for his theme of light and darkness.

For the Lesson:

Aim: To see what a candle does in the darkness.

Materials: A beautiful white candle in a simple but artistic holder. A taper with which to light the candle or a long matchstick. A well–wrought candle extinguisher—preferably one that can be cleaned and shined by the children at another time. A special place in the room to put the candle.

Conversation: Gather the children around you and darken the room. Ask them what happens when it gets dark. "Can you see one another?" "Can you find your way?" "Why do we like light?" Place the candle in the center of the group and slowly light it with a taper. "Look at the candle." "What happened to the room?" "To our faces?" "Look at the flame." "What color or colors is it?" "If I hold my hand close to it, what happens?" (Remember you do not need to ask all these questions. The children will begin to make these observations spontaneously.) Hold up the candle and move it, asking them to follow the light with their eyes. Then tell them, "We will follow the light with our eyes, hands, feet and even our hearts."

Activity: Walk in front of the group with the candle, singing a song about fire or light. Place the candle in a special spot, extinguish it, and go back to work. (Notice in this walk we have made use of the game, Follow the Leader.)

MANY CANDLES

Give each child a small candle and call each one by name to come and take light from the large candle. Say, "Now, see how much light there is!" "Notice whether the large candle lost any light or not."

LIGHT FROM A FIREPLACE

Many things can be learned when sitting around a fireplace. Where does the smoke go? What happens to the logs? (They are transformed to flames and then to ashes when they are burnt out. Teach the children the word transformed.) Ask, "How do we feel sitting around the fire?"

SLIDES AND PICTURES

Use slides or photographs. Extend the notion of light and fire to a sunrise or sunset. Notice the death and life-giving notions inherent in the idea of fire. It can be destructive: it can cause explosions or burn people.

SUGGESTED READINGS

Books

Dreikurs, Rudolf. *Psychology in the Classroom.* New York: Harper and Row, 1957.
Fromm, Erich. *The Art of Loving.* New York: Bantam, 1962.
Getman, C. N., and Kane, Elmer R. *The Physiology of Readiness.* Minneapolis: P.A.S.S., 1964. (See especially the Overview.)
Ginott, Haim C. *Between Parent and Child.* New York: Macmillan, 1965.
Harris, Maria. *Dance of the Spirit.* New York: Bantam Books, 1988. (See especially Chapter 1.)
Montessori, Maria. *Discovery of the Child.* India: Kalakshetra Publications, 1962. (See especially Chapter 24.)
Nelson, Jane. *Positive Discipline.* New York: Ballantine Books, 1987.

8 The Sensitive Periods

Chapter 7 dealt with the discipline of children, explaining how we can help children achieve self–discipline by feeding their intellects, bodies, and emotions. In it we suggested that children be led to understand what the good of all is. We spoke about the Montessori Silence Game and presented the biblical images of light and fire.

In this chapter we want to present a lesson on seeds and to give the rationale for our approach.

Young children are fascinated by and sensitive to the things of nature. This is their first meeting with nature and they are in wonder at all they see. Montessori had a name for certain periods in development in which the child seems sensitive to certain stimuli in the environment. She called these stages "sensitive periods."

THE SENSITIVE PERIODS

In observing little children, Montessori found that there were times in their development when they seemed extra–sensitive to sound and to movement. She reasoned that this sensitivity gave children the motivation necessary to master certain tasks, such as speech. She divided the sensitivity periods into age groupings. She called the child from birth to three years of age the "unconscious learner." During this period the child is especially sensitive to language, to order, to details, and to movements. From three to six years of age the child's sense of touch, the ability to adapt to different individuals, the religious sense, the inquiring hand, the senses of taste and smell, can all be observed as indications of inner sensitivity.

CHILD DEVELOPMENT IN THE HOME

These periods of sensitivity are observable not only in a Montessori classroom but in the home as well. Parents have wondered about the exasperating tendency their children may have to pull all the pots and pans out of a cupboard and then rearrange them. But this activity might well be encouraged. The child is showing a need to put the visible world in order. In the nightly ritual of going to bed, the three–year–old child wants to be tucked in, have the light turned off, and drink a glass of water. We know what happens when this order is reversed. How many times have parents said, "Must you touch everything?" The answer is, "Yes." This is the way the child learns shapes. Parents should observe this development and in doing so learn to feed their child's sensitivity.

The child should also be allowed to learn from others. Often, as we said before, a playmate knows what a friend wants and how to give it. We have observed one child help another to stop stuttering. As you watch two children look at a picture of a big pussy cat against a background of trees and flowers, you will find them talking not about the pussy cat but about the tiny flower in the comer of the page. This shows a sensitivity to details. For this reason we do not feel that the seed, our next biblical image, is too tiny an object to whet the child's curiosity.

THE SYMBOLISM OF THE SEED

In ancient civilizations, the seed was symbolic of hidden forces. In order to insure a good harvest, people held fertility rites in honor of the gods. In the Old Testament we find the Israelites, who had for a long time lived a nomadic life, settled down to a life of raising crops. As they settled, they came in contact with the fertility rites of neighboring people. The Passover feast is an example of an Israelite feast that was influenced by the neighboring harvest feast. But the Passover feast became for the Jews the remembrance of much more than thanksgiving for a harvest. It was a time to offer thanks to God for bringing them out of slavery and making them chosen people. All the ceremonies the Jews performed, although they resembled non-Jewish rites, were no longer thought of as heathenish, but as a proclamation of their salvation, the Exodus from Egypt.

At the time of the New Testament, God's Son took the same ancient feast of grain and gave it a meaning it never had before. Christ, the only Son, the first fruit, the Paschal Lamb, was the seed that fell into the ground and brought forth new life. This connection of the feast of

Nurturing Your Child's Spirit

the Passover with Christ's own death and resurrection is emphasized in the Gospel of St. John. He tells us that at the time of the celebration of the feast, when crowds had come to Jerusalem, Christ said, "Very truly, I tell you, unless a grain of wheat falls into the earth and dies, it remains just a single grain; but if it dies, it bears much fruit. Those who love their life lose it, and those who hate their life in this world will keep it for eternal life " (John 12:24, 25). Christ was about to make the great passover to His Father—the great action which would make it possible for all humanity to be brought to the Father through Christ. Christ conquered death once and for all. He provided a way out of death.

One of the things that concerns children is death. It is a great mystery to them, as it is for all mankind. This was brought home to me when our nation was in mourning for President Kennedy. The children came to school filled with all they had seen on television and heard from their parents about this great tragedy. It was terrible. It was all over. President Kennedy was dead. One child said with finality, "He's dead I tell you. I saw the dirt and the fire on top of the dirt." I searched to give him an answer. I wanted to say, "No, President Kennedy is in heaven," but I knew the child would ask, "Where is heaven?" I did not feel that I had an answer that would satisfy the child. Finally, I took a seed we had planted. We had already talked about the seed dying and the new life which was there. This time I dug a small hole in a pot of dirt and said, "This is like what happened to the President. You see, the old seed is dying, but look! There is a new life. President Kennedy was buried in the ground but his life was changed, not taken away. President Kennedy went to a new life." I think the child—and I—gathered from this experience a new insight into the mystery of death.

And so a tiny thing like a seed can tell us of hidden life. It can tell us that life must die to give new life. It can remind us of Christ who died and rose to new life in order that we may have life and have it more abundantly.

CONCLUSION

In this section, we have suggested a way to help children understand one of the greatest mysteries of life, the meaning of death. We have not concentrated on its painful aspects, because we have looked toward the direction and meaning Christ has given it. In our lesson we will bring in one of the other ideas that we have already learned, the notion of growth and life from water.

We suggest that you plant wheat seeds, because in another lesson we will demonstrate how bread is made from grains of wheat. This is a preparation for our understanding of the Lord's Supper, where bread was broken and life given. In all these experiences we have tried to respect the inner growth and development of the child. That is why this chapter stressed Montessori's notions of sensitive periods.

LESSON

Seeds

General Objective:

To help the child to have a beginning understanding of death.

For the Parent and the Teacher:

Aim: The death of a seed and its gift of new life can remind us of Christ's words, "Unless the seed dies." This action, then, reminds us of the death, resurrection, and ascension of Christ in which we are joined at the celebration of the Lord's Supper.

Background: Christ also used the symbol of a seed in the Parable of the Sower to speak of the word of God sown in the hearts of men. (Mark 4:1–9; Matt. 13: 1–9; Luke 8:4–8). The seed is compared to Christ and his action. This lesson on the death of a seed is a preparation for considering the more complicated parable. Do not teach the parable until you are sure that the child can follow a sequence of the four types of growth of a seed: by the path, in rocky ground, amidst thorns, and in good soil. This may be done after walking together and looking for plants and how they grow. The important thing to stress here is the law of growth. All growth involves pain, a breaking out from the old, change. Joy can come after suffering. Before we are willing to risk change we must have some assurance of the goal. In the formation of the faith life of an individuals, religious educators can only witness to this by their own conviction and through analogy. Finally, it is only the faith experience of the truth that reveals to the Christians what they have learned from hearing. For we can only give the possibility for this experience of transcendence.

For the Lesson:

Aim: A seed can remind us of a new life through death.

Material: Culture dishes of seeds in various stages of growth. Seeds of various kinds in and out of their shells. A pot of dirt, a small spade on a tray, and a watering can.

Conversation: This is an especially good lesson for individual work and conversation. But it may also be conducted as a group lesson. In either case it should be broken up into three parts.

1. Take an apple (or some other fruit), nuts, soybean pods, or similar plants and ask the child to cut or break the fruit open. Examine the seeds within and talk about what you find. If you use an apple, cut it up so it can be eaten at the end of the conversation. Before doing so, you may sing:

   "The Lord is good to me
   And so I thank the Lord . . . "
   —"Johnny Appleseed Song" from Walt Disney's *Melody Time.*

2. At another time, take a large seed such as a pumpkin or lima bean seed and place it on moist cotton. Note that the seed shrivels and a new sprout forms. Note also the roots.

3. At a later time take a pot of dirt and slowly dig a hole and place a growing seed in the dirt. The conversation during this time may be about death and burial, but say, "There is a new life." Flash cards with the children's names on them to indicate when they may come and look at the seed. This is a variation of the Silence Game and of the call–and–response activity that is the prayerful activity of the Christian's life. Prayer is a response to God's call in Scripture, in the life of the community, and in the things of nature. The response is one of leaving all to follow Him (John 1:39). It includes an identification with Christ—a dying and a rising.

Activity: There is much activity in the above section. However, children may be occupied quietly by planting their own seeds which they will cultivate and water. Other activities should include the separating of seeds into dishes as suggested with rocks. The children may do this blindfolded to develop their sense of touch. These activities can be opportunities for conversation and growth.

Wheat Seed I

General Objective:

To talk about the planting of a specific seed, a grain of wheat.

For the Parent and the Teacher:

Aim: To understand the importance of cereal offering in the Old Testament and thereby learn its connection with the offering of bread at the Eucharist.

Background: The grain seed is one of the basic products of Israel (grain, wheat, and oil). The wheat seed is grown during the winter and reaped in March and April. Note that the Passover season coincides with this harvest. Thus, it was natural that the Israelites would imitate their neighbor's harvest festivals and offer cereal in thanksgiving not only for a good harvest but in remembrance of the great passover into the Promised Land. It was then that they were given life, freedom, and a new beginning.

Christ's death took place during the commemoration of this feast. He was the cereal offering. His passing over to the Father wrought our freedom, our new life, and our new beginning. Christ was the new covenant with God. We are assured of everlasting access to God. We have stability, security, assurance of salvation. Our act of offering bread is in great thanksgiving for Christ's deed. We join our lives with His in this act.

There were other offerings in the Old Testament that were acts of sacrifice. We have spoken of the offering of first fruits. Christ was truly the first fruit in which was contained all of his members. Others rituals included the eating of a meal and the burnt offering. Later there were rituals of atonement. The most common ritual was the sacred meal.

For the Lesson:

Aim: The wheat seed can remind us of new life through death.

Materials: Grains of wheat and small pots of dirt, perhaps one for each child. A set of small garden tools placed on a tray with a sprinkling can of water. A small orange stick with the word "wheat" on one side and the name of the child on the other.

Conversation and Activity: Pass the wheat seeds around and ask, "What must we do if we want to grow wheat?" "What happens to the wheat when it grows?" (The seed dies and there is a new life.) Show the children how to dig a small hole or furrow and scatter the seeds into it. Describe how seeds were planted in the time of Jesus and how they are planted now. Use pictures for this. Water the newly planted seeds and talk about the effects of water.

Give each child a pot of dirt and an orange stick. Let the children plant the seeds now or have one child demonstrate how to plant and let the rest do it in their own time. If you wish to have a more communal activity, ask the children to take turns planting seeds in one pot. Do not promise that these seeds of wheat will ripen entirely, for it is likely that they will not unless you plant them outdoors. It is enough to see the process of planting and the harvesting for them to experience the growth and maturation of the wheat. You may sing any one of the songs we have learned or read a story about wheat. (See *The Little Grain of Wheat*, Gerard Pottebaum.)

Wheat Seed II

General Objective:

To learn that it takes many grains of wheat to make bread.

For the Parent and the Teacher:

Aim: To understand the eucharistic symbolism of grinding wheat into flour.

Background: Christ is the bread of life whose offering of himself to the Father makes him present to us as the source of life. We have seen the meaning of passing over into a new life through death and burial. We have seen that suffering can bear fruit. Christ's words, "Unless the seed die," are explicit. The same idea is present in the symbolism of grinding wheat to make bread. The wheat must surrender its present form in order to be made into a form that gives life. This change involves crushing and grinding.

Shortly after Christ's death, his disciples understood how their transformation into him would take place. The persecutions showed them that they must be "able to drink the cup" that he drank (Matt. 20:22). Christ's disciples celebrated the breaking of the bread and remembered the meaning of the grain of wheat. As early as 110 a.d. St. Ignatius of Antioch, the second successor to the apostle Peter in the See of Antioch, compared his own death—being torn by wild beasts—to the grinding of wheat. When he heard the roar of the lions he cried out, "I am a kernel of wheat for Christ. I must be ground by the teeth of beasts to be found bread [of Christ] wholly pure" (*The Church's Year of Grace*, by Dr. Pius Parsch, p. 435).

This early witness to Christ wrote seven famous letters on the way to his death, which give us a great knowledge of the early church's consciousness of Christ and his word. He wrote to the Romans, "It is God's Bread I want, the Bread from heaven, the Bread of Life, which is the Flesh of Jesus Christ, the Son of God . . ." (ibid. p. 437). As a bishop, Ignatius was concerned about the unity of his flock. Exhorting them in an epistle he said, "Be concerned about each other. Strive together, walk and suffer and take your rest together, rise together . . ." (ibid. p. 437). Apparently Ignatius's words about the grinding of wheat could include the meaning of many grains making the one bread—that it is together that we overcome evil. He wrote to the Ephesians, "See to it that you come together very frequently to celebrate the Eucharist of God and to praise His name. For, if you come together often, Satan's power is broken, and his pernicious influence destroyed by your concern in the faith" (ibid. p. 441).

One of the earliest prayers of the church, from the Didache, "The Teaching of the Twelve Apostles," written before the end of the first century, expresses the same thoughts: "As the elements of this broken bread, once scattered over the mountains were gathered together and made one, so may your Church be built up from the ends of the earth and gathered into your kingdom" (ibid.).

For the Lesson:

Aim: To observe what happens when we grind many grains of wheat.

Materials: A dish and a tool to grind with. This may be a small apothecary mortar and pestle or even an electric mixer. A bag of wheat seeds on a tray, and, possibly, a bag of wheat flour, to show the children a larger amount of flour than you have time to grind. Pictures of flour mills, even millstones can be discussed if there is time.

Conversation: Pass around the wheat seeds and discuss what you have learned thus far. Invite the children to eat a grain of wheat. (Remember, this is what the disciples did once when they were hungry. They did it on a Sabbath and Jesus had to explain the correctness of this act to the Pharisees.) Let them see that it is tasty and good to eat.

Pass around the tools for grinding and name them. Then slowly pour some grains of wheat into the bowl and begin to grind.

Invite the children to take turns grinding. Discuss the flour that appears after awhile. (You may now show them the pictures of flour mills or else save them for another lesson.) Ask, "How many grains are needed to make flour?" "What must be done in order to get the real benefit of the seeds?" (They need to be destroyed but they are really brought to a new form.)

Activity: Your "grist mill" could be set up in the room for the children to use whenever they wish.

SUGGESTED READINGS

Books

Guillet, Jacques. *Themes of the Bible.* Notre Dame, Ind.: Fides Publishers Association, 1960. (See especially Chapter 6.)

Montessori, Maria. *The Absorbent Mind.* India: The Theosophical Publishing House, 1961. (See especially Chapter 11.)

Parsch, Dr. Pius. *The Church's Year of Grace.* Collegeville, Miun.: Liturgical Press, 1962.

Pottebaum, Gerard. *The Little Grain of Wheat.* Dayton, Ohio: Pflam (Little People's Paperbacks), 1964.

9   Education of the Senses

Chapter 8 was given over to a discussion of the sensitive periods of a child's life. In it we noted the child's sensitivity to small details and presented a lesson on a very small item, a seed. In this chapter we wish to continue the discussion of the education of the senses and to explain the materials used in the lesson.

SENSORY EDUCATION

From the beginning of our discussions we have stressed the fact that children learn through their sense impressions. That is why we use concrete objects. However, there is in what Montessori called "sense education" something more than indiscriminate physical contact. Montessori often tried to achieve sensory education through the refinement of the senses. This is why, for example, a Montessori teacher introduces the child not only to the primary colors but to the various shades of red, green, and yellow. The Montessori teacher plays games with the children, teaching them to refine their color sense by grading colors from dark red to light pink, or from dark green to light green. As we implied in our discussion of the periods of sensitivity in the child, such a task is easy for a child. At the same time Montessori desired a creation of order and clarity in the child's sense impressions. The grading of shades of colors not only refines the child's sensitivity to these colors, but also helps clarify the differences in shades and the order of these differences.

CREATION OF ORDER AND CLARITY IN SENSE IMPRESSIONS

Sensory education requires special materials. We have already talked about these as "didactic materials." Such materials improve children's perceptions by enabling them to isolate the various qualities and to grade them. The brown stairs, mentioned in Chapter 4, teach children to place in order rectangular solids of increasing width and depth. The children arrange them in order of size. By using the same materials they can also compare the largest of the set with the smallest to understand the idea of contrasts.

Built into each set of materials is what Montessori called a "control of error." If the brown stairs are not in proper order children who have been taught to sit back and look at their completed work will notice what is out of place. The control of error is provided not only in the materials but also by the teacher who simply presents the lesson to the children again, showing them the correct way to use the materials.

SELECTION OF PROPER MATERIALS

What can be learned from this about religious education? Perhaps the greatest thing we can learn is discrimination and proper sequence in the selection and use of materials. Here are some suggestions to keep in mind: First, always present three–dimensional objects before pictures. Before reading a story and showing pictures of the parable of the grain of wheat, for example, show the children a grain of wheat and what happens to it when it is planted in the ground. Too often we omit an important step by going too quickly to the story and pictures. Second (and similarly), a child should actually experience something before hearing about it. How do we come to a knowledge of the Trinity? Does not the church bring us first to this knowledge through the experience of the sacraments? Through the church we experience the Spirit of the Father and Christ's love. Through Christ we know his Father and his Spirit. Third, isolate that which is to be taught. In other words, take one thing at a time. Montessori talks about points of interest. To teach children to tie their shoes, the teacher must slowly demonstrate each step in the process. What do children learn from visiting a zoo if parents rush them through every building? Would it not be better to see the fish one Sunday and then the tigers or reptiles on another Sunday?

In this lesson, we are going to discuss the table. We suggest that the children be gathered around a table. On it we will place a rock, a candle, and one plant. In this way we will place together what we have experienced separately.

THE SYMBOLISM OF THE TABLE

Why is a table so important to us? Because we gather around it to eat together. For the ancients, eating had a sacred meaning. Some sacrifices were offered on an altar that was looked upon as a table where the gods and goddesses ate. Ancient people constantly tried to come into contact with the divine, so it is not surprising that they made of eating a ritual way of communicating with a god. Often the sacrifice was burned because it was thought that the gods consumed the sacrifice by inhaling rather than by chewing it. It is not difficult for us now to imagine eating together as making an agreement. When we accept an invitation to eat with someone we are indicating an agreement with the other. A good salesperson knows a deal is almost closed if a customer agrees to lunch.

At the time of God's recorded acts in history the Jewish people came into contact with God primarily through a sacred meal. It was in this way that the Hebrews offered thanks for life. A gift of first fruits or an unblemished animal was offered. Part of it was burned—transformed from the profane into the sacred—in order that it might be given to God. The other part was eaten by the people. We have already mentioned the feast of the Passover, a great meal of thanksgiving, commemorating God's act of delivering the Hebrews from slavery. During the meal the people remembered all that God had done for them and once again pledged their loyalty, thus renewing the covenant of agreement that they had made.

Christ took this meal of thanksgiving and gave it a new meaning. "Then he took a loaf of bread, and when he had given thanks, he broke it and gave it to them saying, 'This is my body, which is being given for you. Do this in remembrance of me.' And he did the same with the cup after supper, saying, 'This cup that is poured out for you is the new covenant in my blood.'" (Luke 22:19–20). Christ, who had spent himself giving light, life, and health to all he met, now, on this solemn occasion, gave and promised to pour out his blood in order that a new covenant with God might be made. Now when we eat together we remember not only the deliverance from slavery of old, but the deliverance and the gift of new life given through Christ, the promised one. Christ took the most ordinary action by which we keep ourselves alive, the action of eating, and transformed it into a means of coming into everlasting life.

Every meal that we eat together can be a reminder and a preparation for the sacred eating together at the Eucharist. To eat properly, we give and receive. At the table of the Lord we give and receive Christ.

In a Montessori classroom much attention is given to eating together. Everyday the children learn to serve one another with exquisite courtesy. Watching this, one is struck by the similarity of these activities to the eating of the bread of life at Eucharist. The children serve one another. Did not Christ give an example of service at the Last Supper?

The children wait for one another before beginning to eat. Is this not an opportunity for becoming aware of each other as members of the group? The children sing a song of thanks. Is this not a recognition of our dependence on God? Eating together is not only receiving and giving food. The courtesy that accompanies this act, the pleasant chatter, are not these a giving and receiving? And when we are together at the Eucharist, and we are united to Christ, are we not giving and receiving one another in the celebration of the Lord's Supper?

Obviously, a class of twenty–two children cannot sit at one table. For this reason, the children sit in a circle on the floor or arrange their tables in a circle. This is where parents are at a great advantage. At home there is a table around which the family gathers. The father may sit at the head of the table. He is a leader and a giver of life to the children. He begins the prayer of thanks. It would be good for the father or the mother to make up an appropriate prayer of thanks on special days. This would be a more meaningful way of expressing what is happening at home. In this prayer the parent can first thank God, mentioning special blessings received, and then ask God to satisfy the family's special needs and the needs of the world through his Son and Spirit with whom we wish to live forever.

We do not always need to fold our hands to pray—we can lift them upwards with arms outstretched. This is perhaps a more natural way to express the fact that we are open, giving, and receiving in this act of eating. Holding our hands upward is a gesture of surrender. Is this not what we do when we reach out to God? Perhaps this seems a strange thing to do in the home. If so, it is not necessary to do it. It is only suggested as one way to make meaningful the gestures of the Eucharist and relate them to everyday life. The suggestions in these lessons are not meant as hard and fast rules. They are meant only to help you think creatively about what can be done together in the family.

LESSON

The Table

General Objective:

To give the child a background for understanding the table of the Lord.

For the Parent and the Teacher:

Aim: A table can remind us of Christ who is "our altar" (Heb. 13:10), the place of contact between God and humans, "offered once for all" (Heb. 9:28) on Calvary and with whom we unite at the commemoration of this sacrifice at the Lord's Supper.

Background: In the lesson on wheat we spoke of three types of rituals of sacrifice in the Old Testament. The most common was the sacred meal. This required some kind of table at which the people and God met. It is significant that the image of a mountain preceded the altar image as a place where one could contact the divine. Notice the combination of images in this verse of Isaiah, "But you who forsake the Lord, who forget my holy mountain, who set a table for Fortune and fill cups of mixed wine for Destiny" (Isa. 65:11).

Now Christ becomes this holy mountain, this place of contact, this covenant, this table of the Lord. It is around him that we gather, and are we united through him. Christ is the center of our lives. We come to the Creator through him. It is at the Eucharist that we meet, are fed, and come into the most profound contact with God.

Finally, after the resurrection, Christ walked and talked with two disciples who were downcast. They asked him to stay with them. St. Luke points out that, "he was at the table with them, he took bread, blessed and broke it, and gave it to them. And their eyes were opened, and they recognized him . . . then they told what had happened on the road, and how he had been made known to them in the breaking of the bread" (Luke 24:30–31, 35). This is what happens when we meet at the table of the Lord. We recognize ourselves as we truly are—children of God, brothers and sisters in Christ. Truly we are known to each other in the breaking of the bread.

For the Lesson:

Aim: To gather together at the table of the Lord.

Materials: Select a small table that is simple and not too big to be handled by two small children. Have a place set aside for it when it is not in use. In the home situation it should be your regular dining table that you point out to the children. In a classroom one small table will have to serve as a reminder of the ones we can all gather around. Have on the side a white tablecloth, napkins, candles, a beverage, and a snack.

Conversation and Activity: Sit in a circle at some distance from the bare table. Discuss the use of the table, how it holds God's gifts to us, gathers us together, serves as a place where we can meet. Try to bring together many of the notions that we have already discussed. Ask, "Remember how we said we could meet under a tree?" "Can a rock be a table?" "We are a community when we gather around the table." "How do we act at the table?" "How do we serve one another?" (Remember how Christ served at the Last Supper). You may ask a child to demonstrate how one pulls out a chair to sit at a table. "What do we do at the table?" Explain again the meaning of life-giving water that we drink at the table.

Show the children how we dress the table for special occasions. Carefully unfold a tablecloth and arrange it. Place the napkins and a snack on the table in buffet style. In the home this is more beautifully done when the children learn how to set the entire table. Place the candle or candles on the table. Ask the children to sit around the table and sing a thank-you hymn. Then serve them from the table.

N.B. This lesson may be broken up into several small lessons:

1. Lesson on dusting a table

2. Lesson on setting a table

3. Lesson on learning how to sit at a table

4. Lesson on talking together at a table

5. Lesson on serving at a table

This table lesson could well be called a culmination lesson of the above five.

SUGGESTED READING

Book

Montessori, Maria. *Montessori Method.* New York: Schocken, 1964. (See especially Chapter 12.)

10 Religious Psychology of the Child

In the last chapter we spoke about gathering around a table. We pointed out that this has many possibilities for helping the child to understand what happens when the people of God gather around the table of the Lord to give and receive Christ. We said that the courtesy expected of the children at the table is reminiscent of our Lord's own act of service to his friends. This activity combined the lessons we had on rock, water, and seed. Some of these objects were placed on the table and we gathered around again to sing a song of thanks.

The first part of the chapter spoke about Maria Montessori's notion of sensory education and gave some principles for the selection of materials for religious education. We stated that the child should experience objects before seeing pictures of them, that experience should precede words, and that we should isolate points of interest in order to make the presentation clear to the child.

RELIGIOUS REALITIES

Perhaps you have wondered why we did not speak of showing the child a picture of our Lord. We did not do so because of one of the principles just outlined: a child should confront objects before pictures. There is another reason that has some bearing on this: Children should be given every opportunity to picture Jesus in their own way. Often we move in too soon and give children a stereotyped image that limits their imagination and may perhaps stop them from having a much better idea of what Jesus looks like than an artist could ever depict. Indeed, we have spoken of Jesus by singing his name and likening him to a tree, a light, a rock. If it is true that we are united to Christ as branches to a vine, then is it not possible that by sitting in a circle looking at one another we get an idea of what Christ looked like? Christ became the

Christ we know through one another. He has eyes, a smile, hands, feet. We are united to him. Are we not living signs of his presence to us?

Acting upon these ideas, I tried this in a Montessori classroom. I did not show the children a picture of Christ for about three months. One day four little boys got into a conversation about whether Christ was Superman. When they came to me with the problem, I answered that Christ was the king and Lord of all. One little fellow asked "What does he look like?" I paused for a moment and then looked at the four boys and said, "When I see Bryan smile, then I get an idea of what Christ looks like." The boys began to look first at Bryan and then at each other. They smiled in order to see what Christ looks like. This was a very real experience that helped us to understand the mystery of the mystical body of Christ.

Later I found a picture of Christ that I thought suitable and decided to show it to the children. The picture I chose was that of the risen Lord. The reason for this is that Christ, our Lord, is present to us now in his risen state. It is not Christ in the crib or on the cross who abides with us through the power of the Holy Spirit, but Christ fixed forever in the fullness of his resurrection. It would be well for the child's first representation of Christ to be one which depicts him as he is in glory. The message of the apostles to all was that Jesus is alive. This was the good news upon which all their hopes were based. St. Paul said, "if Christ has not been raised, then our proclamation has been in vain and your faith has been in vain" (1 Cor. 15:14).

What does Christ look like? Who is Christ? Christ is the One who has conquered. He is the One who has come into full possession of that for which we strive—humanity fully free, fully saved, in full relationship with the Creator and with each other. This is the Christ who is present with us at the Lord's Supper. This is the Christ who is present wherever there are two or three gathered together in his name.

In order to prepare a child for a real encounter with Christ we must necessarily be selective. This is one of the principles we spoke of in the last chapter. Our selection depends not only on the psychology of the child but on the very selection the apostles made when they began to preach. For this reason we have selected "four realities" that should constantly be revealed to the child. The first of these is the love of God, witnessed to by the love of a husband for his wife and her love for him. St. Paul in the fifth chapter of the Epistle to the Ephesians applies this mystery of matrimony to the church. You need not tell children that God loves them if they constantly see the love of their parents. Children know that love exists, that it is fruitful, that they are caught up in it. The second truth is that Christ is the revelation of God to humankind. The risen Christ is present now in our midst, acting through each one of us.

In our love for one another we experience Christ's love. We are growing in Christ to the Father. The third truth is that the actions of Christ bringing us to the Father are continued in his church. It is possible for us to be saved now through the sacraments. The principal sacrament is the Eucharist. There we are united to one another in Christ. The fourth truth is that all of this action has taken place in time, in history. This is salvation history. God's eternal plan of love is being worked out now.

In dealing with children, we must begin with this reality—not with a story, but with the introduction to Christ the Lord as a great person whom we love. Then we gradually let children know that this person loves them, that he did certain things, that he had friends. And then in wonder at his love, the children realize how little they deserve such friendship and become acutely aware when they fail in this friendship, which failing we call sin. We maintain, strongly, that there must be established a friendship before there can be sin. Sins are not merely taboos.

RELIGIOUS PSYCHOLOGY OF THE YOUNG CHILD

This brings us to the final point, the principles of psychology implicit in this program. We must take seriously what psychology tells us about the child under six:

1. The young child does not have a sense of history, of time. Everything happened "last Saturday."
2. A child is totally open to truth. We must be careful of what we tell children, so that it will not be necessary for them to discard later on in life what they learned in their impressionable years.
3. The child has an innate sense of mystery.
4. The child has a sense of ritual. This is why children make up little rituals for themselves. They seek order in all they do.
5. The affective life of the child is the avenue of learning. It is only in a loving, warm atmosphere that a child can receive the truths of the surrounding world.
6. The child is attracted by adults and prefers them to babies. Though fascinated, the child will not imitate babies. That is why we prefer to show a child a picture of Jesus as a man.
7. The child is capable of generosity, offerings, and so forth. When children will not give up something they possess, it is because they see it as part of themselves. We must respect this need for identification and not call it selfishness.
8. The child imitates perfectly. This is why a teacher must be an exemplar. The child must be able to imitate one who is ever striving to be a good Christian.

In the lesson, we will talk with the children about Christ our leader. Christ asked his disciples, "'Who do people say the Son of Man is?'" and they said, 'Some say John the Baptist, but others Elijah.'" Finally, Simon Peter said, "You are the Messiah, the Son of the living God" (Matt. 16:14, 16). We make this confession of faith each time we acknowledge Christ in offering to him the daily work of our lives. In all this children are prepared for the action of the Eucharist. There they will communicate with the person of the risen Lord by giving themselves as they join with others and bread is offered.

There is one thing which cuts us off from giving our gift at the altar. That is sin. Christ said, "So when you are offering your gift at the altar, if you remember that your brother or sister has something against you, leave your gift there before the altar and go first be reconciled to your brother or sister, and then come and offer your gift" (Matt. 5:23–24). In our culture, we may punish children by asking them to go to their rooms and not eat with the family. We stated earlier that sin was the breaking of a relationship, and that there must be friendship before there can be sin. Previously we discussed the development of children in terms of their learning to relate to others. We suggested that children who are uncooperative be isolated from the rest in order to get a better perspective of what it means to work within a group. We also sang together many times and experienced the oneness of community, of silence, of praying together. We told a little boy that when he sees another child smile he gets an idea of what Christ looks like. All this may be called the formation of conscience, the ability to judge what is right and wrong. Only when children experience friendship, relationship with parents and brothers and sisters, can they become aware of what it means to deliberately break this bond. (The question of sin and confession will be taken up in more detail in Appendix I.)

A Montessori teacher was sitting with a group of children preparing to eat with them when one of them began to misbehave. She quietly took his juice and cracker from him and put them away. She did not scold the child. He no longer belonged. He had cut himself off from the group. Later she talked with him about this. He replied, "I hate to say this. I really hate to say this, but my mother said to tell you that I am sorry." She replied very warmly, "I forgive you." Then, it seems, the child saw a smile that helped him to know what Christ looks like, and began to understand forgiveness.

1. A Picture of the Risen Lord

General Objective:

To help children to know Christ, the risen Lord.

For the Parent and the Teacher:

Aim: To show a child a picture of the risen Lord formally for the first time.

Background: Most of what we want to think about is contained in the previous section. Although we have not yet shown the children a picture of the risen Lord or any picture of Christ, this does not mean we have not given them an image of the Lord. All the things we have tasted, touched, smelled, and looked at have given us an idea of Christ. Most of all our contacts with each other tell us of the person of Christ. Christ is our brother, our friend, a fellow son of our heavenly Father.

We ask you now to turn to a flat, two–dimensional representation of Christ, a good, artistic, picture of the risen Lord. We choose this event of Christ's life because it represents his victory over death. Christ is still risen and in our midst. St. Paul says this forcefully, "if Christ has not been raised, then our proclamation has been in vain and your faith has been in vain" (1 Cor. 15:14). The fact of the resurrection is the truth upon which everything we believe rests. When the Father accepted Christ's death, he raised him from the dead. The resurrection is the sign of the acceptance of Christ's sacrifice. We know we are saved through the resurrection. We celebrate the event of the resurrection each Sunday. We rise, dress, and go to church to sing with joy of Christ's victory over death. Small children should have happy experiences of getting ready to celebrate with their parents. Sunday is special. It is the celebration of all that we have spoken of in our previous lessons. Sunday celebrates our new life from water, baptism, our loving of one another, the faithfulness of God, the promise of happiness together forever in a new life in heaven.

For the Lesson:

Materials: A table, a tablecloth, candles, flowers, an attractive empty dish, a covered picture of the risen Lord.

Conversation and Activity: Ask the children to help you fix up the table. Spread the cloth and light the candles. Tell them you have something special to place on the table. Place an empty dish on the table.

Now show the children that you have something covered up. Tell them or ask them how we have spoken of the Lord and who he is. Ask the children to name some things that remind them of the Lord. Then tell then that people remind you of Christ and what he looked like. Tell them that you have a picture that was painted by an artist who tried to tell what he thought Christ looked like. Remind the child that the Lord is more beautiful than any picture. Then unveil the picture and place it near the candles and flowers on the table. Try to have an interval of silence so that the children can reflect on what they see. You need not discuss the resurrection.

Point to the empty dish on the table. Ask the children to make or draw something and place it in the dish as a gift for the Lord. You may wish to remind them that we have offered gifts before when we decorated a tree that reminds us of Christ and when we celebrated birthdays.

The children may be left to offer the gifts on their own, or, more formally, you may sing a song as they do so.

2. A Song with the Picture

General Objective:

To deepen the understanding of the risen Lord.

For the Parent and the Teacher:

Aim: To present the risen Lord through a picture.

Background: We must first remember that none of us knows what Christ looks like as he is now. The apostles, especially St. Paul, experienced the presence of the risen Lord. Matthew, Mark, and Luke described their own experience of the risen Lord when they described his transfiguration before Peter, St. James, and John prior to his death. Perhaps this is the best source from which to get a description of Christ as he is now. Mark says that Christ was transfigured before Peter, James, and John, that his garments became glistening, intensely white. He said that they were exceedingly afraid and that a cloud overshadowed them. They heard a voice saying, "'This is my Son, the Beloved . . .'

Suddenly, when they looked around, saw no one with them any more, but only Jesus" (Mark 9:7).

This does not seem to be a very detailed description of Christ in glory for our children who want to see a face and hair and hands and feet. St. John's description of Christ speaks of him as "a Son of Man, clothed with a long robe and with a golden sash across his chest. His head and his hair were white as white wool, white as snow; his eyes were like a flame of fire; his feet were like burnished bronze, refined as in a furnace, and his voice was like the sound of many waters" (Rev. 1:14). We may read these things and we should. And, yet, as we read them, we realize the impossibility of picturing a person such as Christ, who has been drawn into full relationship with God. These ideas, coupled with the idea that we see the risen Christ's body when we see his members, our brothers and sisters throughout the world, suggest to us that as we attempt to show representations of Christ, we must remember the mystery and the promise of the vision to come.

For this reason we selected a photograph of a man on a beach and asked a mother to show it to her children. She merely told her children that this was a picture of a man on a beach, with outstretched arms. The children talked about the water. One child raised his arms up high in imitation of the man in this picture. The mother told the children that this might be one way of thinking about Christ who is present here with us now. She stressed that we do not know how beautiful he is and we can only try with photographs and paintings to image him.

We suggest this approach because we feel that we must be honest with our children and tell them as soon as we can how difficult it is to visualize the risen Christ. If we tell them that, and yet we show them by our attitude and convictions that Christ is with us and Christ is for us, then we and our children will attempt to grow in our understanding of Christ.

Two important principles are involved here. First, we are preparing the children by giving them a foundation which they can build on rather than something they will discard later on as childish. This is important in any science or field of knowledge. A child must never be given an illusion of reality. A child should never learn something that must be unlearned later on. You may feel that this approach would make the child insecure. It seems that this kind of insecurity is the only authentic approach to the mystery of Christ. We do not have an answer. We have only the hope of the promise that God has made, the God who is as faithful as a rock.

The second important principle is that both you and your child must look together at this mystery of our salvation. This is the best method of learning in any situation. Teacher and student work together to find the answers. In this way we may help a child to continue the search and to come to a real discovery of the meaning of life.

We hope that after this presentation the child will have some sense of the presence of Christ and will grow up knowing that the presence of other Christians is an assurance of the presence of Christ. "Now we see in a mirror dimly, but then we will see face to face" (1 Cor. 13:12).

For the Lesson:

Aim: To explain the picture.

Material: A photograph of a man dancing or in some posture which connotes "glory." We used a photograph showing the silhouette of a man standing on a beach and facing the rising sun. You may choose another kind of photo, for example, a picture of a ballet dancer, or an athlete.

Conversation and Activity: See above.

3. FLOWERS AND THE RESURRECTION

General Objective:

To deepen the child's experience of the risen Lord through the experience of flowers.

For the Parent and the Teacher:

Aim: To use flowers that appeal to the senses of touch, smell, and sight as symbols of the beauty of the Lord who has risen from the dead.

Background: There are many beautiful artificial flowers available for use in the home. They look almost real. However, for little children who are being introduced to the real world, we should use real flowers. For this reason, cut flowers, which need water to live, which depend on the warmth of the sun's rays in order to grow and blossom, which grow up with weeds and are dependent on our Creator's care, may become a symbol to all children of God, and of our dependence on God for our final glory.

Flowers are signs of celebration. Flowers can be reminders of the risen Lord in our midst, Whose face shines "like the sun, and his clothes . . . dazzling white" (Matt. 17:2). Christ talked about flowers. "Consider how the lilies grow; they neither toil nor spin, yet I say to you that not even Solomon in all his glory was arrayed like one of these" (Luke 12:27).

Flowers are a sign of God's care and of our dependence on Him. We must not worry or be anxious; God knows we have needs. Christ talked about this soon after he had taught the apostles to pray the Lord's Prayer, "Give us this day our daily bread" (Matt. 6:11). Christ said "daily" rather than monthly. In the Old Testament when the daily bread of manna fell from the heavens to feed the Israelites, they were allowed to gather only enough for one day. God was teaching the Israelites to depend on their Creator. Finally, Christ became the true bread which came down from heaven to feed us.

For the Lesson:

Aim: To arrange flowers attractively so that they will speak to the child of the risen Lord.

Materials: Cut flowers, a tray with scissors, a vase, watering can, and a sponge.

Conversation: You need not be as formal as the materials may indicate, but if you do arrange flowers with the children, then all your utensils should be ready so that the children can work efficiently. Show the children how to trim the stem and place the flower in the vase. Show them how to stand back and appraise the arrangement each time they put in a flower. As you work, take one flower and admire its beauty. Gently pull the petals apart and show the tiny stamen and the arrangement of the petals. Show how each flower differs from others of its kind. Talk about variety and beauty. Try to find a color in the house as vivid and pure as the color of the flower. If it is springtime talk about how good it is to see the flowers after the long wait of winter.

If the children remain interested, tell them that the flower can remind us of Christ who came into a desert world to give us life. Talk about the beauty of the flower, and how it does nothing to take care of itself. (This is especially true of wild flowers.) Ask the children, "Who takes care of wild flowers?" Then teach the children, "Give us this day our daily bread."

Remember that this lesson can be repeated several times before all these ideas are learned. As the children's understanding increases, tell them stories from the Old Testament that show how the people had to learn to trust in God. Do not forget the sign of water that is present in this lesson. Ask the children again what water means. Be sure also to let the children work with the flowers after your demonstration.

4. An Ivy plant: The Vine and the Branches

General Objective

To present the idea of Christ the vine, we the branches, by using an ivy plant.

For the Parent and the Teacher:

Aim: By watching and caring for an ivy plant we can help the child to see how a relationship to Christ is like the closeness of branches to a vine.

Background: In our first lesson, we gathered around a tree that reminded us of Christ. We spoke about this as a symbol of the source of our life. We talked about other symbols—water, a rock, light, a seed—and saw how these things remind us of Christ. Finally, we looked at a picture of the risen Lord.

In this lesson we will experience something that Christ identified with himself, a vine. Christ said, "I am the true vine, and my Father is the vine grower. He removes every branch in me that bears no fruit. Every branch that bears fruit he prunes to make it bear more fruit" (John 15:1–2).

In the Old Testament, the people of God were often called vines or were compared to vineyards that need to be tended to bring forth fruit. The prophet said, "Israel is a luxuriant vine that yields its fruit." The people of Israel understood how carefully a vine had to be tended and pruned if it were to bear fruit. They understood that God's punishments were ways of pruning them so that they could bear fruit. Stories about vineyards were written to show the people that God was acting for them. Isaiah related a parable about a vineyard that yielded no fruit, so the master had to destroy it. In this way Isaiah warned the people of what would happen to them if they did not repent of their ways (Isa. 5:1–7). Christ told another parable about a vineyard that had good fruit but whose tenants would not let the master's servants or even the master's own son harvest the fruit. The vineyard in this case was the kingdom of God that would be given to any nation bearing fruit.

Finally, when Christ called himself the vine he was saying not only that he bore good fruit but that he was the head of the new Israel, the faithful Israel, and that all the members were as close to him as branches to a vine. Christ made it clear that one could not live separated from the vine. This is central to our faith. Christ is at the center of our lives. He gives us life. We respond as believers—loving others as he loves us.

There are three things to be learned by experiencing the meaning of a vine. First, branches must be attached to the vine in order to live. The life of the vine must abide in the branches and can only do so by union. Second, the vine must bear good fruit in order to be worthy. It is not enough to say "Lord, Lord." Third, every vine must be pruned if it is to bear good fruit. To live in Christ, one must be willing to accept the total message of divine truth, which purges and cleanses.

For the Lesson:

Aim: To teach the child how to care for a vine so that he will appreciate the vine.

Materials: A potted vine and utensils to dig and water it. Pictures of vineyards.

Conversation: Show the children how to care for a vine. They will be able to tell you why water is important. Now you can stress the need for cultivation. If there are brown leaves, pull them off and ask them why this is done. Be sure to name the parts of the vine: "vine" and "branches." Repeat these names, because you are building a language for understanding the biblical parable. Ask the children or demonstrate to them what happens when you break off a branch.

If the children are ready, tell them that the vine can remind us of Christ and that we are the branches. Ask the children to name some branches. Now you can talk to the children about the necessity of being close to the vine.

Activity: Show some pictures of grape vineyards and explain how important it is that these vineyards bear good fruit. Be sure to use the word "fruit" as often as you use the word "grapes." If you wish, you can talk about winemaking.

Now that you have a table on which you can place things, place the vine on it near the picture of the risen Lord.

11 Children and the Liturgy

In Chapter 10 we discussed the use of a picture of the risen Lord. We used a picture of Christ as he is now because it is difficult for young children to know the difference between yesterday and tomorrow. Everything is now. We proposed using this time in the children's lives when they do not have a sense of history to give them the idea that Christ is now, present to us in his glory.

In this chapter, we will present a lesson on the word of God, which speaks more effectively than any image. As preparation for this, we want to consider words in general and a technique Montessori used in teaching words. Martin Mayer, in his book *The Schools* writes that language to children is a tool employed to impose themselves upon their environment. If we are to help children to grasp the meaning of reality, then our first task is to help them to use the words through which they can express their understanding. One technique is the three-period lesson developed by the French psychologist Seguin and used by Montessori.

LANGUAGE AND THE THREE-PERIOD LESSON

In the three-period lesson, the teacher simply shows a child an object and says, "This is blue." Then the teacher takes an object of another color and says, "This is red." This is the first period of the three-period lesson. The teacher then repeats the names of these colors without adding further description, in order to isolate the one aspect of the object to be taught. During the second period, the teacher says the words again and listens to the child repeat them. Pausing for a few seconds, the teacher asks, "Which is red?" "Which is blue?" Notice two things about this second period. First, the instructor asks about the colors, but in such a way that she or he is repeating their names. Often this repetition of words is overlooked and it becomes difficult for the child to remember the correct word. Second, in order to ensure the child's success, the teacher asks the question repeating the name of the color just mentioned. Thus if the teacher has just said, "This is red," she or he will ask, "Which is red?" This period may be repeated many times. The teacher will vary it by saying, "Give me the red one," or, "Take the red one and put it on the table." By introducing movement the teacher takes advantage of the child's tendency to learn through motion. The test of what the child has learned comes in the third period when the teacher asks, "What is this?" If the child identifies the color correctly, the teacher moves on to two other words.

THE WORD IN OUR FAITH

What bearing does this have on religion? Simply this: In order for children to impose themselves upon their environment with the understanding that comes from faith, they must be able to use the language of faith. We have already said that we need not be afraid to use the correct words for naming things. Children love big words. After children have experienced eating together, for example, we may say, "This is community," a notion that will be treated in Chapter 12. As the child's experience expands to include a visit to church we should correctly name such things as "baptistery," "altar," "candles," and "table of the Lord's Supper." We can do this effectively by teaching the names by means of the three-period lesson described above.

THE SYMBOLISM OF THE WORD

Words hold a fascination for everyone. For people in ancient times, the word was not only an expression of thoughts or will, but it was active also. The word, especially someone's name, held a certain power. This idea is often at the basis of magic formulas. In Old Testament times the power of a word came from God. One of the best examples of the power of the word of God can be found in the prophecy of Isaiah. Here the Lord says, "For as the rain and the snow come down from heaven, and do not return there until they have watered the earth, making it bring forth and sprout, giving seed to the sower and bread to the eater, so shall my word be that goes out from my mouth; it shall not return to me empty, but it shall accomplish that which I purpose, and succeed in the thing for which I sent it. (Isa. 55:10–11). God's word proceeds from God and does as God wishes.

Christ came forth from the Father as the Word. St. John says, "And the Word became flesh, and lived among us, and we have seen his glory . . . " (John 1:14). Later on when Jesus called himself the true bread from heaven he said, "The words that I have spoken to you are spirit and life" (John 6:63). Simon Peter affirmed this, saying, "Lord, to whom shall we go? You have the words of everlasting life, We have come to believe and to know that you are the Holy One" (John 6:68–69). Christ, the Word of God, speaks words that give life. We must learn to listen, to be open to them in order that we may have life.

PRAYER

If young children are to grow up into Christ, they must come into union with the Father through Christ. We call this prayer. A person can communicate with another person and grow into union with that person through conversation because in this way two persons may share the same kind of thoughts. A time may come when they can share the same thoughts without using a great many words. The point is that if there is to be union and growth, there must be a sharing of consciousness. Apparently, this was what St. Paul meant when he said that we should put on the mind of Christ. We teach our children to pray not so that they can learn a way of getting what they want, but so that they can learn to grow up in Christ, and, in this friendship, put on the mind of Christ.

If praying is a putting on the consciousness of Christ, then the best way to teach children to pray is by helping them listen to what the Creator God is saying through Christ. This is really listening to the Spirit. Already, through some of the concepts presented in this book, we have been helping children listen to the words of Christ through the things in our everyday lives that remind us of him. We have also mentioned various words from the Bible through which children can learn to understand and thereby know what God is saying. The possibility for prayer has been given to the children many times through the songs which we have sung, through the gesture of lifting the hands, and through conversations. It is especially through children's conversation with their parents or friends that they meet Christ—for all Christians are a sign of Christ and Christ speaks through them. All these things have prepared the children for the privileged moment of prayer when they participate in the sacraments, especially the Eucharist.

In this chapter we will give the child an experience of real listening, of hearing the word of God. We will darken the room, light a candle, and maintain silence so that the powerful words of the Bible can be heard. When we gather around the table of the Lord we come into communion with him not only by eating the bread but by opening ourselves and listening to the word. Both actions deepen our union with Christ.

The first words that we will proclaim to the children are those Christ spoke to his disciples on the night before he died. In this discourse, Christ spoke of himself as the vine and promised to send the Holy Spirit to be a comforter and guide to his church. Read Christ's words of comfort for yourself (John 14–17).

Children see their parents reading the daily paper and discover that this is the way they learn the news of the day. What about the sight of a mother and father reading the word of God and finding out the good news of every day?

What an opportune moment for meeting and hearing the word of God when a child asks, "What are you reading about?" In many churches, the Bible has a special place of honor. We might take a child to a church to see just this.

With this introduction to the word of God, and with the background of the signs of life presented in this book, parents and teachers should be ready to pray with their children in many different ways. Perhaps after a Eucharist, at which you have heard the word of God and when it has meant something special to you in terms of your own particular concerns, you can remember the passage and say it again before dinner for your children, as grace before the meal. This passage need not be long, but it should be meaningful. You will know by listening to the word of God, to your own family, and to yourself what text would be best for you to repeat for your children as prayer.

Or, it may be that your child will be singing a song around the house or repeating a passage from the word of God that he or she has heard or read. Without pushing, you can take another look at or listen again to these words, and just before eating, or when the child is going to bed, use these words as a prayer. Often we find ourselves quoting the word of God. Sometimes in a moment of distress or a moment of joy, without being pretentious, we can say them again to our children. This is prayer.

Another suggestion for parents and teachers is to make up a prayer. We could call this "spontaneous prayer." The prayer you make up might have three sections. The first part could consist of words of thanks and praise to the Creator God. The second part could contain words that reveal how much we need and are dependent on God. The third part might say to God that we know we receive all things through Christ and the Holy Spirit. The following is a type of a prayer that includes these three sections:

Father or Mother: Loving God, we thank you for having brought us together today.

1. We thank you for (mention something that happened recently for which you are grateful).

2. We ask you today to help us (mention needs).

3. We pray this through Jesus Christ who lives with you in the unity of your Spirit, now and forever.

All the children: Amen.

We suggest that you try to help your children in their petitions so that they can truly grow up. Prayer is not a means of getting things from God. Rather, prayer is a putting on the consciousness of a friend to whom we tell our needs, acknowledge our dependence and wait in love for this friend to answer us. God, who is like a father and mother to us, knows our needs and has asked us to reveal our needs. It might be good for your children to listen to your intentions first, so they do not get into the habit of praying for strange things.

In considering a more formal way of praying, we suggest that parents pray the Lord's Prayer a phrase at a time with their children. We cannot suggest when to pray it, or which specific phrase to use because this must be determined by the situation. It is important, though, to say the Lord's Prayer in this way rather than to have children learn the entire prayer without knowing what they are saying. Children will be going to the Eucharist with their parents and they will hear the community saying the entire prayer. They can be prepared to hear the people of God say these words, if their parents say just a few of the words with them at times of conversation. Perhaps one evening during prayer before she goes to bed, the parent may say, "Nancy, let us pray together to God so that mother and dad and all the family will be what we should be for the world. Just say these words after me, 'Thy will be done on earth as it is in heaven.'"

LESSON

The Word of God

General Objective:

To learn that Christ our Lord said some significant things and that they are written in the Bible and called the word of God.

For the Parent and the Teacher:

Aim: To understand why we "listen" to the word of God.

Background: The important thing to remember is that the word of God or Revelation cónsists of God telling us who God is, and a testimony to the actions of God in history. These words are so powerful that when listened to in faith they are a source of life.

The child should learn to listen to the sounds of words. We should read the words reverently. The many lessons we have had should prepare the child to understand the words, and that the course of our lives is directed by them. We know how to confront life properly, we know who we are and Who Christ is when we have listened to these words.

For the Lesson:

Aim: To help the child "listen" to the word of God.

Materials: A table, the Bible, a pillow for the Bible, candles.

Conversation and Activity: Begin the lesson by telling the children that Jesus said some things that are written down. Usually this will surprise them. Then show them the Bible and tell them that it has many names. Write on a blackboard or on a piece of paper the names, "Holy Bible," "Word of God," "Good News." If three are too many, then choose just one of the three, preferably "Word of God."

Let the children reverently open the Bible only after you have shown them how to do it. Let them take their time. Then, when they are quiet, ask them to listen while you read something Jesus said. It may be best to lead into the particular passage with a few introductory sentences of your own such as, "Jesus told us how close we must be to him." He said:

> "I am the vine, you are the branches. Those who abide in me, and I in them, bear much fruit because apart from me you can do nothing" (John 15:5).

Close the book quietly and sit still for awhile. It is best not to try to explain anything. Your actions will tell the children that this is important, and that is enough. However, should the children wish to comment on the passage then take this cue from them and discuss what you have read. If there are several children, form a little parade or procession with two children carrying the candles, another child carrying the pillow, and another carrying the Bible. If there are more children, each one might carry a flower. Be sure to have vases ready to receive them. Walk to the table singing a song. Place everything on the table. This activity should be repeated many times.

OTHER PRAYERS ON THE WORD

Many passages from the Bible can be used as prayers. You will note that they deal with themes that have already been presented in this book.

Tree

Let anyone who has an ear listen to what the Spirit is saying to the churches. To everyone who conquers I give permission to eat from the tree of life that is in the paradise of God (Rev. 2:7).

Water

As the deer longs for flowing streams,
  so my soul longs for you, O God.
My soul thirsts for God,
  for the living God (Ps. 42:1–2).

The LORD is my shepherd, I shall not want.
  He makes me lie down in green pastures;
he leads me beside still waters;
  he restores my soul (Ps. 23:1–3).

Rock

I love you, O LORD, my strength.
The LORD is my rock, my fortress, and my deliverer,
  my God, my rock in whom I take refuge,
  my shield, and the horn of my salvation, my stronghold (Ps. 18:1–2).

. . . and all ate the same spiritual food, and all drank the same spiritual drink. For they drank from the spiritual rock that followed them, and the rock was Christ. Nevertheless, God was not pleased with most of them, and they were struck down in the wilderness (1 Cor. 10:3–5).

Light

. . . to give light to those who sit in darkness and in the shadow of death, to guide our feet into the way of peace (Luke 1:79).

God said, "Let there be light," and there was light. And God saw that the light was good, and God separated the light from the darkness. God called the light Day, and the darkness he called Night. And there was evening and morning, the first day (Gen. 1:3).

Seed

Unless the grain of wheat falls into the ground and dies, it remains alone. But if it dies, it brings forth much fruit. He who loves his life, loses it; and he who hates his life in this world, keeps it unto life ever-lasting (John 12:24–25).

When a very great crowd gathered and people from town after town came to him, he said in a parable: "The sower went out to sow his seed; and as he sowed, some seed fell on the path and was trampled on, and the birds of the air ate it up. Some fell on the rock; and as soon as it grew up, it withered for lack of moisture. Some fell among the thorns, and the thorns grew with it and choked it. And other seed fell upon good ground and sprang up and yielded fruit a hundredfold (Luke 8:4–8).

Community

Because there is one bread we who are many are one body, for we all partake of the one bread (1 Cor. 10:17).

[Jesus Christ] will also strengthen you to the end, so that you may be blameless on the day of our Lord Jesus Christ. God, is faithful; by him you were called into the fellowship of his Son, Jesus Christ our Lord (1 Cor. 1:8–9).

Table

When he was reclined at the table with them, he took bread; blessed and broke it, and gave it to them (Luke 24:30).

FLOWERS

The wilderness and the dry land shall be glad,
the desert shall rejoice and blossom (Isa. 35:1).

A BLESSING

The LORD bless you and keep you. The LORD make his face shine upon you, and be gracious to you. The LORD lift up his countenance upon you, and give you peace (Num. 6:24–26).

SUGGESTED READINGS

Books

Mayer, Martin. *The Schools.* New York: Harper, 1961.
Montessori, Maria. *Montessori Method.* New York: Schocken, 1964.
    (See especially Chapter 12.)

12 Liturgy and Celebration

In Chapter 9 we suggested that we place on a table some of the things of nature that can tell us about our relationship to God. These might have been placed on a shelf or on the floor, but the emphasis was on the special meaning that gathering around a table has for us. It is there that we come together and are strengthened. In Chapter 10 we spoke of images of the risen Lord who is present in all our gatherings. In Chapter 11 we listened to the Word of God with the child. All these activities are religious. In each meeting with elements of the universe we can begin to answer the basic question of life: "What is the meaning of my existence?" If the answer can speak of ultimate reality in such a way that what has been handed down of old can be heard today, a truly human existence is made possible. When we cannot find any meaning in life, boredom, despair, lack of interest, and aimless wandering are the results.

LITURGY

It is not enough, however, to have private talks with children or adults to help them understand their relationship with the world. Their existence cannot be assured in this way alone. Rather, children, as well as adults, must celebrate their existence.

This celebration of existence is the liturgy. John Dewey said that art is the extension of the power of rites and ceremonies to unite human beings, through a shared celebration, to all incidents and scenes of life. The liturgy properly takes up this celebration. In this union, however, it is not merely human beings who communicate. Through the celebrant, the person of Christ, the person of the Father and the person of the Holy Spirit speak and act toward us. We are together.

What makes this communication possible? How can we have a

liturgy for children? How can we have a liturgy at all? First of all, liturgy is formed by taking the elements of the world and letting them speak. Some of these elements are cosmic symbols. The presence of water, tree, fire, and rock, either in their natural forms or in an art form, calls to each of us and speaks to us of life.

The second aspect of a liturgy is the range of symbolism on a psychological level, the level of experience. An experience is made possible through the presence of art forms that speak to the whole person. We have already mentioned this in the use of cosmic signs. In this chapter we will include some suggestions concerning the use of music as an art form that speaks to the whole person.

Listening to music and singing together can unite us. The music we use must, therefore, not be foreign to everyday life. When individuals gather together to be strengthened in their understanding of the meaning of life, they cannot be helped to do so by music that is strange to their ears. The child of today toddles in front of a television set that uses background music made up of electronic sounds, of strong beats, and close intervals.

Another art form that provides the possibility of an experience and the means to communicate is gesture. The perfect symbol, the one that communicates perfectly the invisible, is the body. The gestures of the human body sometimes tell more about an individual than anything said. For this reason the lessons presented often use gestures, for gestures involve the whole person and help the person to express the invisible.

The third aspect of a liturgy is its social symbolism. This is the actual relation of a child to others. Throughout this book we have tried to suggest ways to help children toward an awareness of others. The Montessori Silence Game, the ground rules concerning the respect for another's work, the reverence with which a child is taught to handle objects, serving one another—all make possible a gradual development toward social activity. This is the perfect way to prepare a child to participate in the liturgy. Worship on Sundays does not compensate for lack of concern for a neighbor during the week. When we meet to be strengthened, we must truly meet and not stand apart.

Most properly, the liturgy of which we speak is the Eucharistic meal. How can this solemn celebration speak to children? So far we have tried to help by teaching children how to understand the signs that are present: table, candles, words. In this chapter we are going to discuss the notion of community, the symbolism of breaking bread, and then, on the basis of all that we have learned, put together a liturgy for children.

To help us understand liturgy, and especially this great coming together at the Lord's table, we must first experience what it means to be together. When ancient civilizations wished to come into contact with the divine they did it in a ritual—a special dance, a song, a gesture. The tribal chief led his people in community worship. In the Old Testament the Lord called his people out of Egypt, gathered them together, and, through a patriarch who acted in their name, made a special agreement or covenant with them. The Lord through his prophet said, "you shall be my people, and I will be your God" (Ezek. 36:28). The people of the Old Testament were keenly aware of this because they saw that when one of them did wrong the guilt experienced had repercussions in the whole community. They felt a solidarity, a oneness, in reward and punishment.

It is this same oneness that Christ spoke of when the time of the New Covenant, the New Testament came. We have seen that Christ called himself the vine, and us the branches. The Father raised up Jesus as one with whom we could all be united, as a vine is united to its branches. Later St. Paul spoke of this community, this fellowship. To try to explain it, St. Paul used the image of a body, and said that we were one body and Christ is the head (Eph. 1).

To understand this concretely we must experience being together. Singing together, eating together, working together—all these activities give us an idea of what it means to be one in Christ. There are many images we can use to express this. Many grains of wheat making one bread demonstrates this well. But what about our bodies? Is not sitting in a circle with hands joined together a more total way to experience community?

In the lesson, we suggest that you demonstrate community to children by showing them a sculpture or pictures of people together in a circle. (The sculpture we suggest using was executed by Margie Gregg. It is called "Community," and is available from the Glenmary Sisters, P. O. Box 22264, Owensboro, Kentucky, 42304.) You can talk about the statue or the pictures and then name the grouping "community." Say the word. It has four syllables. Do not let that frighten you. Children are fascinated by words. They really do not care for baby talk. Write the word on a card to show them what it looks like. It is good to expose them to whole words. They are used to seeing big words on the television screen. We would not consider turning the television off because the words are too big. This is a part of their environment. After they have said the word, you can sing about community.

SINGING IN COMMUNITY

Singing is a community-forming activity. It is interesting to note that Montessori suggested that the teacher use a stringed instrument to accompany the voice, not only because it most closely resembles the human voice but because it enables the teacher to face the children. This approach is important for children's first introduction to singing together. It helps them to experience singing as a form of communication.

We suggest using antiphonal songs. This means that the teacher sings (or calls) to the children and the children answer with a short response. This prepares the children for congregational singing in church.

It is important that the children's response be spontaneous. Rather than telling them what the words of the song are instructing them to do, the teacher should ask them to listen and then wait for them to act out the song. Not all children will respond in this way, but each child should be allowed to participate as an individual. The acts of sitting and listening may be a very real way of participation. The teacher may act out the words, but in such a way that it neither inhibits nor forces the actions of the children. In order to learn to harmonize you must learn to listen to the harmony and not hold your ears closed. Do not introduce harmony to the children until you are quite certain they will succeed in holding the sustaining note. This is true of rounds also.

BREAKING BREAD IN COMMUNITY

Like singing, breaking bread is a community-forming activity. We have said that ancient people made a ritual of eating with the gods, and that even today eating together is a way of saying that we are in agreement. Thus, eating has a covenant meaning. This is especially true of breaking bread. In the Old Testament, one broke bread as a sign of friendship. This was done especially after a pact had been made with someone. The phrase "breaking of bread" was a specifically Jewish expression originally meaning the beginning of a meal and then later the meal itself. After asking a blessing, the head of the family would begin the meal by breaking bread and giving a piece to each person at the table. Since bread was the principal food, the expression "to break bread with someone" came to mean sharing a common meal.

Christ followed this Jewish custom. He did this when he multiplied the loaves. St. Matthew records it in this way: "Taking the five loaves and the two fish, he looked up to heaven, and blessed and broke the loaves, and gave them to the disciples" (Matt. 14:19–20). All accounts of the Last

Supper stress the introductory part that consisted of giving thanks and breaking bread. Christ broke bread and gave it to the apostles to eat.

It is important that we see the celebration of the Eucharist in the same way that Christ and his disciples saw it: once again we are breaking bread and eating together in a feast that unites us with one another and with Christ. This cannot be stressed enough. We do not go to worship alone. This writer remembers asking a little child some questions to see whether he really wanted to go up to the altar for Communion. He waited for awhile and said, "Yes, but not alone." The breaking and sharing of bread is a community-forming action. "No," we said, "your mother and father and all of us will be with you and you will be closer to your mother and father than you have ever been before." St. Paul said, "Because there is one bread, we who are many, are one body, for we all partake of the one bread" (1 Cor. 10:17).

Let us consider the lesson on breaking bread. We have already ground some wheat into flour to show that many grains make one bread. Now we are ready to mix wheat flour, oil, salt, baking powder, sugar, and water to make wheat patties that we will then bake and eat together while singing a song such as, "Let Us Break Bread Together."

There are many other things that can be done with children to prepare them for the Eucharist. We might crush grapes and make wine, or let the children examine a chalice, the cup of the Lord. It is not suggested that you go into detail or require the children to memorize the parts of the Eucharist, for this makes them concerned more for the mechanics of the service than for the celebration. You may do it later on, when the child wishes to be more precise. However, just now the child is at a stage of wonder, of romance, and this precious time should be used in the best possible way.

We have not discussed the liturgical year. One reason for this omission is that a child does not have a sense of history. In addition, we want to emphasize that we are now in the last age, the time of Christ's fulfillment of the promises made to Abraham and Sarah. Each Sunday we celebrate Christ's resurrection and we recall only the events that led up to it. There are ways to remember these events that do not cloud the idea of Christ's risen presence in our midst. For example, one family brought home palms from the Palm Sunday celebration and had a little parade in honor of Christ our King. Christmas is a time to celebrate the fact that Jesus is the living Christ for us. On All Saints Day, we remember those who have conquered death with Christ and who celebrate the eternal banquet of heaven while waiting for us to join them. Every feast of the Blessed Virgin Mary can remind us that she is the mother of Christ who is present to us now.

Every year, we celebrate something that could easily lead the child to an understanding of liturgy. That is the child's birthday, the day when the three- or four-year-old is the center of attention. At this celebration, we can give gifts and thank God for giving this life to us, for otherwise we would not know the child. Once we appreciate the gift of life, then we can appreciate the gift of life given in Baptism. Baptismal days and patronal feast days are celebrations that can be part of our everyday lives only if we see them as coming out of everyday life. We are merely following the dictum, "Grace builds on nature," when we try to appreciate what it is that we live everyday and see how it is directed to the day that will never end when we enter into new life with God in heaven.

A CELEBRATION FOR CHILDREN

On the basis of all that we have tried to communicate to the children, we are now ready to give them the possibility of experiencing oneness with all, and, through Christ and his Spirit, oneness with the Creator God. This is what we mean by a children's liturgy. We want to give the children an experience in which they can begin to understand the meaning of life in a most profound "privileged moment." This is the Christian message. This is revelation. This privileged moment is the celebration of thanksgiving for life that we call the Eucharist. It is the Lord's Supper, the ritual meal in which we remember the agreement God has made and kept with humankind.

In this section we will summarize the Eucharist as the totality of Christian revelation. What does this mean? It means that if all the signs in the world can reveal Christ and if Christ is the sign or self-revelation of the Father, then the Eucharistic celebration, when we meet Christ in an experience made possible through signs, is the whole of Christian revelation.

In this section we propose more than a lesson or the possibility of an experience. We propose a celebration of the Lord's Supper as the culminating experience of your work with children. At present, we allow children to attend the Eucharist on Sunday with the family in order to have them learn its meaning. In many places small children go daily to the eucharistic celebration. We are not proposing a radical departure from these practices. Rather we ask that you decide for yourself, in the light of what we have presented thus far, what the best way is for your child to come to understand the meaning of this profound act.

Since the most important part of the eucharistic celebration is the breaking of bread, we suggest that every decision about how to break bread with a child be concerned with making this sign understandable. What we are about to suggest is something we hope will occur when Eucharist in the homes and experimentation are more commonplace. We can enjoy a similar experience now by having a service of breaking bread. The children's Eucharist could incorporate these suggestions and could be celebrated in a room suited to them. Ideally, the first part of the Eucharist is a time of greeting the children, a time to relax together with a song and then, after a moment of silence, to listen to a familiar passage from Scripture. The best place for children to listen would be in the living room, on the floor, or seated next to their parents. Then, if it seems opportune, the family might discuss spontaneously the words read. Perhaps the children will suggest another song. Perhaps someone will offer a prayer. The leader of the celebration should gather up these elements of song and prayer and speak about them, "preaching" in a manner suited to the occasion.

For the second part of the celebration, everyone might be seated around the table while the mother or father and the children set the table, bringing the offerings of bread and wine and lighting the candles. The celebrant then would lead the group in remembering Christ's death, resurrection, and ascension, and thanking God for the gifts of bread and wine. After breaking bread and offering the sacrament, the celebrant would drink this holy wine and ask all to drink it with him, passing it around in one cup or pouring it into wine glasses. Prayers and songs of thanksgiving might be offered after this.

A third part of the celebration might be setting the table for a special festive meal. There are a few points to remember when planning this culminating experience. First, it is important that the children meet the celebrant many times before the celebration, becoming their friend. Then, there should be a continuity of thought in the songs and in the readings. Try to use the same songs, the same readings from the word of God. It is these same songs and these same words that will carry the experience which the children had into this final, culminating experience. Third, the actions should be the same as they have been in the lessons we have presented. Gather in a circle around the same table, or sit comfortably on the floor. A gesture of joined hands during the song is a natural symbol that creates community. This, then, is fitting for the celebration of the Lord's sign of unity. Let the child speak to you, walk around, be at home during this happy celebration. These, too, are signs of friendship.

Finally, in order to help children become aware of the last blessing, if there is one, you might call their names and invite them to come and receive a blessing. This can also be done at the time of breaking bread.

This gives each child a chance to hear his name called and to respond. This is the action of the Christian's entire life. The Christian is responding to the call of God.

LESSONS

1. Community

General Objective:

To have the child experience the meaning of community as oneness.

For the Parent and the Teacher:

Aim: The most intense experience of community is the meaningful participation in the action of the Lord's Supper. Here Christians join themselves to one another and to Christ and become one as members of God's family.

Background: St. Paul is our best source for the meaning of community. Read especially the Epistle to the Ephesians.

For the Lesson:

Aim: Community means we are one.

Materials: A covered copy of the sculpture, "Community," or some other piece that represents a group together. Tag board or paper to write the words "*community, many, one.*"

Conversation: After you have directed the children's attention to the covered sculpture or picture, uncover it and look at it for awhile.

Invite the children to touch the sculpture or to look at the picture. Use the tag boards to identify the many in the one group. Then tell them that the name of this group is "Community." Write it on a tag board. Say it together.

Ask the children to look at themselves. Ask, "What are you doing?" Sitting in a circle. "What happens when you put your arms around each other?" "What can we name ourselves?" Write down any names they say: class, children, group, set, community, family.

Activity: Sing a song about being together and act out the verses. Sit in a circle and have juice and cookies together. By now the rule should be established that anyone who disturbs the group cannot stay with the group. If a child misbehaves, ask him or her to leave the community. Do so in an even tone of voice. If the child asks pardon later on, be forgiving. One should experience ex-communication—leaving the community, and reconciliation—return to the community. This may happen again at other times.

2. A Birthday

General Objective:

To make the children glad that they were born and that others were born, because if they had not been, we would not know them.

For the Parent and the Teacher:

Aim: To understand that a proper appreciation of our birth prepares us to understand our rebirth in Baptism.

Background: Think about the mystery of birth, the giving of life, the bringing forth of an individual. Every person cries out, "What is it to be?" The answer comes when the individual finds a person who will accept his or her existence. A person is only a person when in relation to someone. We are accepted and rejected each day, and must be able to experience both. But the first experience must be one of acceptance. If we appreciate our birth we can appreciate our Baptism. We cannot understand the wonder of having a Father in heaven if we do not acknowledge the life given us by our parents.

The teacher should keep in mind the significance of making gifts and giving them in a procession to the King as we did at Christmas. This time we will be making gifts for a birthday child. The action this time is different, however, for now the child gives a gift to the other children in return.

For the Lesson:

Aim: To understand what a birthday can mean.

Materials: A canister with gumdrops and other candies in it. Small birthday candles in clay secured to the top of the canister. A taper to light the candles. Materials arranged so that the children can make something for the birthday child. Be prepared to place the birthday child in the center of the group of children in a special chair with a table in front of him so that he can receive the gifts.

Conversation and Activity: If the birthday child has not already announced that it is his birthday, then tell each child individually, suggesting that each one make a gift or card for the child. Do not force the children to do so. When the gifts are finished seat the birthday child at the center of the circle and have the children gather to go forward and present their gifts while singing "Happy Birthday." The last child should carry the canister with the candles fixed to the top. When all are seated around the child, the teacher may ask them to pause a minute while she says, "Thank you loving God for having Johnny born five years ago today. We are glad for now we can know him." Then ask Johnny to blow out the candles. He should then open the canister and distribute candy to each child.

3. Breaking Bread

General Objective:

To help the child understand that we are a community through the breaking of the bread.

For the Parent and the Teacher:

Aim: By making, breaking, and eating bread together we can experience how the holy bread of God makes us one.

Background: The principal things we wish to remember are:

1. Bread reminds us of Christ who called himself the bread from heaven.

2. Bread is a source of life for us just as Christ is our life. We must eat bread daily and partake of the eucharistic bread in order to live.

3. When we break bread at the Lord's Supper we are not alone. We break bread together and in this action we are made one through Christ.

For the Lesson:

Aim: To give the children the experience of making and breaking bread.

Materials: If you are not able to make bread with your child using leaven and other ingredients, we suggest the following method:

1. You will need a hot plate, pan, utensils, and a beautiful platter.

2. Follow this recipe for wheat patties:

1/3 cup 100 percent whole wheat flour

1/3 cup water

1/2 teaspoon baking powder

1 teaspoon sugar

teaspoon salt

1 teaspoon oil

Combine dry ingredients. Add oil and water, and mix until smooth. Pour one tablespoon of batter for each patty onto a greased hot pan and bake until bubbly on top side and light brown on bottom side. Turn patties over and finish baking. Total baking time is six minutes. The recipe yields nine, two-inch patties.

Conversation and Activity: Have the children prepare the table beforehand. Everytime you gather around the table you can ask the children to explain the things that are there. This helps them to realize why we are gathering together, and to understand the meaning of the celebration of the Lord's Supper.

When the patties are finished, break them and distribute them from the table singing an appropriate song. Have the children sit in a circle for this activity.

Sing a song before eating. Do not direct the children to act out the song. Rather, let them do it spontaneously.

4. SIGNS THAT REMIND US OF CHRIST

General Objective:

To communicate to the child that signs speak to us of Christ.

For the Parent and the Teacher:

Aim: To review what the child knows by gathering together a box of things which remind us of Christ.

Background: We have stressed many times that a child can be reminded of Christ's presence by looking at the ordinary things in everyday life. Often we have said, "If the child is ready. . . ." This means that we must wait for the opportune moment to speak about these important things. Some have called this "incidental" teaching. This is the most important kind of teaching, because it arises from the appropriateness of the moment. Religion is not an isolated reality in our lives.

In this lesson we are going to use a method of recall that may be a bit forced and formal. It is more properly a lesson for a school setting. Yet we insert it here to help remind us that we live in a world that is a "box of things." We must remember that we are "lord" in this world. We are made in God's image and act that way insofar as we relate to the world as creators, caretakers, and managers. We glorify God by looking at the world and offering praise. Children must be helped to do this, for they are little "lords" who love to reign in their own small worlds.

For the Lesson:

Aim: To present to the children objects that will help them to understand their relationship to Christ and to the world.

Material: A box containing such things as rocks, seeds, a small candle, and some shells.

Conversation and Activity: Keep the box covered until you have explained that you are going to let the children see some things to talk about. You may wish to blindfold the children who can then place their hands in the box and guess what they have picked out. After the children have identified each object, ask them "What does this remind you of?" By this time you should be able to get some good, precise replies. For example, one child might answer, "A candle reminds me of Christ who is like a light that came into the world." Another, "a shell reminds me of water. When I was baptized water was poured over my head. I received a new life and can grow up with Christ." As a variation you may ask the children to match objects with cards bearing their names. If the children can read, use the cards with sentences explaining how this object tells us of our life with Christ.

SUGGESTED READINGS

Books

Dewey, John. *Art as Experience*. New York: Minton, 1934.

Dodd, Rev. Charles Harold. *The Meaning of Paul for Today*. London: The Swarthmore Press, Ltd., 1920.

Montagne, Ashley. *Man in Process*. Cleveland, Ohio: World Publishing Co., 1961.

Whitehead, Alfred North. *The Aims of Education and Other Essays*. New York: Macmillan, 1929.

Articles

Gelineau, Joseph, S.J. "The Nature and Role of Signs in the Economy of the Covenant," *Worship*, 39, No. 9 (Nov.1965), pp.530–550.

Mead, Margaret. "Ritual Expression of the Cosmic Sense," *Worship*, 40, No.2 (Feb. 1966), pp.66–72.

Schillebeeckx, E., O.P. "Transubstantiation, Transfiguration, and Transignification," *Worship*, 40, No.6 (June 1966).

13 Conclusion

In this book we have tried to give you some things to think about, sing about, and talk about with your child. We do not want to leave you with the impression that children will understand everything you have done together. We have merely attempted to lay a foundation. We wish to appeal to all the senses of young children at a time when they are most perceptive and ready to learn. We are trying to give children something to build on, a basic truth that will be amplified in life, and not a fantasy that will prove untrue later on. We are trying to point children toward what *The Constitution on the Church* calls the "deepest meaning and value of all creation."

FOUNDATIONS FOR RELIGIOUS EDUCATION

Let us try to summarize what we have said about the religious education of the young child. First, a good home relationship gives the child the opportunity to know and love our heavenly Father. A good first seven years with parents helps the child to love and to know others and thus provides the basis for loving and knowing God. Second, there are things in our everyday life that express the love of God for us, leading us into a deeper relationship. These things are symbols such as a tree, water, a rock, fire, a seed, the action of being together in community, and of eating around a table. These symbols and these actions were given special meaning by Christ when he spoke of them and when he came together with his followers. We demonstrated how a child learns to respond to these things in our everyday world and pointed out that this was a response to the call of our loving God in things, actions, and people. We said that we must help the child to build an understanding of these things and thus come to a faith–understanding of life. Third, we said that a child knows of the love of the Father, revealed through his Son, by actions Christ continues in the church. This is why the sacraments are so important. Like anyone else, Christ is known only through his actions and his words. These actions and words are experienced by us each time the church celebrates the sacraments. The most important sacrament is that of the celebration of the Eucharist. Therefore, it is imperative that all we say, or see, or do concerning Christ be connected to the Eucharist.

MONTESSORI'S PRINCIPLES

Every time we spoke of these religious realities we tried to see how the Montessori Method of education might help us to find a way to present them to children. The Montessori Method stresses observation. Maria Montessori said: "Observation is a form of pedagogy." Teachers or parents must be skilled in observation. They must spend time with the child, observing reactions, listening to the clues the child gives. Only then can the teacher know what the child wants to know and how to communicate it. It is through observation that the teacher knows how to guide a child to self–discipline and self–education. We must remember that we can only help a child to salvation, that even God simply calls the child, giving help. The child or the adult must ultimately give a free "Yes" to this call.

We spoke of the place of learning as a prepared environment. Attention must be paid to the environment, the decor, objects that will stimulate interest, and space, sometimes an unpurchasable commodity, but one that is absolutely necessary for the sense of silence. These call forth the emerging personality. This environment provides the possibility for an immersion in experience. Children cannot grow and develop on theoretical notions alone. They must be given rich possibilities for experience. They must be made aware of their place in society. Even lovingly calling their name helps them to know themselves. When they answer to their names, it indicates that they see themselves in relation to others. The acceptance of any work that they do, no matter how meager, is an acceptance of themselves. Then they are created, becoming persons. Children should have their own tables and chairs, their "sacred space." This, too, locates them.

Finally, many of the Montessori principles we have tried to explain can be summarized under the heading discipline. With regard to this, our first concern is relationship. The teacher must have a loving, accepting attitude toward the children so that children will be able to learn to accept themselves. This is the first step to growth or change. This can be accomplished only where there is liberty. Character is built up by free, conscious choices. Each time we give children the opportunity to make choices we are fostering their formation. We are not molders of children. We merely provide the opportunities which will help them to grow. "Let the environment reveal the child, not mold the child," is another Montessori dictum. When giving children choices there must be nothing in our attitude that might sway them; we must help them to make their own discoveries and to stay with the choices they have made. This means we must be willing to take a risk.

We must give children *liberty within limits*. The only limits imposed on children should be the good of the community. Teachers or parents may not ask anything for themselves. They are allies of the children, looking at the world as though beside them, not in front of them. All the work of *self-discipline* begins and ends with *fulfillment of needs*. Deviation, or abnormal behavior, stems from needs within the psychic or emotional life of the child. Find out what is needed, begin to answer the need, feed the emotional life, and the deviations should decrease.

Dr. Mary Pipher, author of *The Shelter of Each Other*, writes about her radical yet standard suggestions for "Rebuilding Our Families." She says, "Watch a sunset, go for a walk or take a trip to a wilderness area . . . I think the natural world has great power to heal and restore broken families" (p. 59).

Another means of discipline is *exercises in control*. Telling children their duties and requiring that they be done, orderliness in returning materials to their proper place, games in muscular control— all help to give children the feeling that they are masters of themselves.

A precaution concerning *corrections* is necessary here. Unless a child is doing something harmful, the teacher should not immediately step in. Then, the correction should be made with the group, in a game–like way, so that the child can discover what is the correct attitude or action. Playing a game of walking without any noise or closing a door quietly, and having everyone take a turn at it, gets the point across with lasting results. Finally, let us say one word about rewards and punishments. There should be none. The joy of accomplishment is its own reward; the sorrow of not accomplishing something, its own punishment.

THE LORD'S SUPPER

All the signs and religious attitudes spoken of in this book seem to find their place most perfectly in the action of the Lord's Supper. As *The Constitution on the Church* states, "The Eucharistic Sacrifice . . . is the fount and summit of the whole Christian life." Through the lesson, we found that at the Lord's Supper we gather around a table, around

Christ who is like a tree. We can remember that we are at the Lord's Supper because we were baptized with water. In our celebration of Christ's death and resurrection at the Eucharist we can realize who the Lord is and say in response, "Yes. Amen." We light candles when we celebrate the Eucharist and realize that Christ is our light in all things. We appreciate together one another's existence because we have been born and called to be children of God. Together, as a family, as a community, we realize that Christ has made us one. We receive a blessing and know that we have been healed. At the Lord's Supper we are reminded that unless we are willing to die with Christ, we cannot come to a new life with him. The Eucharist teaches us to listen, and, by listening, to know who we are and who Christ is. We listen to the words of God and respond. We learn how to have a conversation with a friend. Finally, at the Eucharist we see bread being broken and given to us to eat so that we may live forever.

If we have any hope for the future of our children, let us see that this hope for personal and social fulfillment of the human personality finds its "fount and summit" in the eucharistic sacrifice. If this is so, then the best thing you can do in the religious education of young children is to prepare them to understand what is happening when they participate in the eucharistic sacrifice.

It is with this hope that we have presented for you the ideas here. May we all look to the day when we can meet again, you, your children, and all the children of God, in the eternal banquet of love and joy in heaven.

SUGGESTED READING

Book

Pipher, Mary. *The Shelter of Each Other.* New York: Ballantine Books, 1997.

Appendix I
The Child and the
Sacrament of Penance

This book has said little about the child and the sacrament of Penance. It spoke of the relationship of human beings to God and of sin as the denial of this personal relationship. It does not seem logical, then, to speak of the possibility of breaking a relationship, the possibility of committing sin, until we have given the child every possibility for making the relationship.

This "positive approach" is intrinsic in the Montessori Method of educating the young child. In each set of circumstances the Montessori Method gives practical suggestions to aid the child toward a conscious proper relationship to other people, to the world, and to God. For example, children are allowed to do anything they wish as long as they do not harm the good of all. The child may not touch another's work unless invited, and is assured that no one will disturb his or her work. The simple statement, "This is Mary's; this is yours, makes this clear to the three-year-old. The child learns to respect not only others' work but the things with which they work. The Silence Game, talking together, serving one another, singing together—all these exercises bring about a consciousness of their relatedness.

Such an approach does not deny the existence of sin, nor does it say that every act of the small child is excusable. Rather, it takes a great deal of consciousness—self-awareness—to break a relationship, and this can be called sin. It is necessary that we stay very close to this definition of sin, for without it we find many acts labeled "sinful," which have nothing to do with a religious, Christian level of living. "I broke a glass." "I hit my brother when he punched me in the back." "I lost my library book." "I talked in church." Are these sins, or are they innocent, unintentional acts? It is difficult to say what they are. It can only be said that these acts are not desirable. Karl Stern, in his book *The Third Revolution* states, "We do not like to associate childhood with hatred and destructiveness, yet our reasoning is strangely distorted if we think of the innocent age, the age without guilt, as also the age without evil."

Our problem stems from judging an undesirable act as a sinful act. If we are to understand religion as a relationship, we may judge all things desirable or undesirable only from the point of view of whether they unite or separate us from one another. We judge from the point of view of relationship: "Does this act cut me off from others—from my brother or sister whom I know to be united in Christ?" Such an approach helps us to see that we cannot judge another's act as sinful. We cannot make lists of sins. At best we can speak only of norms of conduct that may or may not be sinful, depending on the individual consciousness.

Should we, then, speak of confession at all? During recent decades at least, the child and the sacrament of Penance has been an important topic, for it presents an area of concern for church leaders, religious educators, and parents. Studies in psychology and theology have helped religious educators to understand that it is not only unnecessary for the child to participate in the sacrament of Penance before First Communion, but that such a practice may actually hinder healthy religious development. Furthermore, although it has been common practice, it has never been required that one go to confession before receiving Holy Communion.

On the other hand, these same studies stress the need for reconciliation between brother and sister. Christ said, "So when you are offering your gift at the altar, if you remember that your brother or sister has something against you, leave your gift there before the altar and go first to be reconciled to your brother and sister, and then come and offer your gift" (Matt. 5:23–24). Apparently, the solution lies in trying to understand the sacrament of Penance and making it a readable sign of reconciliation. This is precisely what the fathers of the Vatican Council have asked: "The rite and formulas for the sacrament of Penance are to be revised so that they more clearly express both the nature and effect of the sacrament" (*The Constitution on the Liturgy*, par. 72).

We, the church, must carry out this injunction. We do this when we make efforts to understand the growth of the human personality and its modes of asking forgiveness. What does this mean? Does it mean that a child shall not go to confession at all? Does it mean that communal activities of asking forgiveness will be worked out for the child's participation? Does it mean general absolution? No one can say just now. All we can say is that in these changing times, we must think in terms of the future and in so doing we will effect a change. Only through a sharing of consciousness by priests, religious educators, and parents can the proper solution to these questions come about. Such sharing in Christ is the work of the Spirit.

PSYCHOLOGY OF THE YOUNG CHILD

In order to further this work in a small way, this Appendix will present some thoughts on the role of the religious educator during the time when the personality of the child is developing. It will also suggest a few practical ways to guide young children. (Many of the ideas in this Appendix have been culled from Louis Monden's book, *Sin, Liberty and Law.*)

In the first chapter of the present book, we said that children operate first on the instinctual level. By the time they are four years old they either have established a sense of basic trust and autonomy, or lack both. It is at this time that they are learning a set of immediate responses to situations that may have little to do with conscious choices. The latter stage of basic autonomy can be compared to Freud's description of the time when children put on a "super ego." Children must learn to fit the cultural setting in which they live. There are certain do's and don't's to living. Children are taught in one way or another that a knife cuts, a glass breaks, or milk spills, and they learn to be careful. Law then is a series of taboos. The child's ego interiorizes pressures from without. At this age, conscience is irrational. Sin, if we may call it that, is a material infringement of some prohibition. Guilt is a blind feeling of activity caused by an action against some order. The feeling of contrition results from an effort to escape the consequences of an act. The resolve is a desire to stay within the limits of the law. Finally, confession can be a kind of magical rite that compensates, in an irrational way for an irrational act.

The second level of development is the moral level, which occurs at about age four to age seven and can be compared to Erikson's description of the stage of the sense of basic initiative when the child begins to come to a curious and reflective consciousness of the surrounding world. Montessori spoke of it as the time when the conscious learner emerges from the unconscious learner. It is at this time that children begin to act in a way that helps them realize themselves as persons. The one basic rule of the Montessori classroom, "You may do as you wish as long as you do not harm the good of all," is for this purpose. When this is uppermost in the teacher's mind, children can be given the opportunity to make decisions that will help them to see themselves in relationship with others.

Thus, law is that which helps self-realization. It guides individuals to give themselves in loving self-donation to others. It is not so much a pressure from without as an urgency from within. Individuals wish to do something in order to be more true to themselves. Conscience is rational. It is a human being's deep self-awareness and even should it err it must be followed. Sin is, among other things, a personal infidelity to oneself in becoming a person. It is an act that results in making the person less a person. Guilt is a subjective feeling that occurs when individuals acknowledge that they have not been true to themselves. Contrition arises from self-reflectiveness. The resolve here is to make up by doing all one can to grow up. Confession, in this case, is not really necessary since the act has essentially been resolved within oneself. Confession is helpful and urged only insofar as it helps in the development of the person.

Before we go to the third level, we must say that young children are just arriving at the second level of action—the moral level—and that no person ever grows out of the level of instinct. In fact, certain instinctive reactions to situations give one freedom of movement, a certain ease within the cultural milieu. The most important point is that if we accept the above description and the definition of sin proposed thus far, we cannot say that the breaking of any taboo or moral code is in itself a sin. Hence, the sacrament of Penance, as we wish to understand it, is not necessarily on the instinctual and moral level. We shall understand this further when we consider the third level of development.

The third level is the religious, Christian level. This level begins when the child is about twelve years old. (It may begin earlier than twelve years, or, as is the case with some personalities it may never begin.) The religious level deals with a person's relationship to someone outside another being, some transcendent person, God, who is manifest to us in Christ through His Spirit. The law of God, then, is not that which helps us to get along, but that which fosters an intimacy with God. The law is love. There will be a growing sensitivity as one lives in union with God. In our work we have shown how there are signs of this love all around us. As we learn to read the signs, we grow in respect and reverence for this Person who touches us through all these signs. Conscience is precisely this growing sensitivity. It is a connaturality, a feeling and thinking with God. Sin is interpersonal, not merely personal. It involves not only a failing against selfdom, but a failing that includes the self and others who are an extension of Christ to the self. It is the breaking of a relationship. Guilt is subjective and objective. There is a feeling of remorse because of this break that is both outside and within. Likewise, contrition is self-reflective and other-reflective. It is an awareness of unfaithfulness to love. The resolve is to do all one can to mend this broken relationship. Since the act concerns someone outside the self, not just another human being, but God, it requires an outward sign or manifestation of reconciliation. This, then, is confession. It is a visible sign of becoming reconciled with brother and sister, or becoming reconciled with the community, which is brought together because of the love of Christ. Now we may ask the questions, "Do we have a practice of confession that speaks this deep reality? If not, what can we do?"

RELIGIOUS EDUCATION AND FORMATION OF CONSCIENCE

The religious educator, parent, or teacher, has a part to play in the life of the young child at the age when reason awakens, between the ages of four and seven. Marc Oraison, the French psychologist, tells us that there is a great deal of difference between a child at the age when reason awakens and the older child who is at the age of free choice (his book is called, *Love or Constraint?*). We are concerned here with what has been termed the age of reason. As we have seen above, this may be more appropriately called the dawn of reason. It is the beginning of growth into free choice. Thus, the religious educator is educating a child for freedom, and is not presupposing that the child is already making free choices. In no way, then, can the religious educator speak of the child's decisions as though they were free, intentional, and deliberate when the child is just beginning to choose. One cannot read to a child a list of possible sins. At the same time, the religious educator cannot ignore the child's attempts to make choices. The religious educator must make attempts to guide the child, to suggest norms of behavior, to lead the child to an ever-increasing awareness of a relationship with others. Threats, condemnations, and judgments distort the child's understanding—they are distorted means. Given every opportunity to understand the manner of acting out love, the child will be most perfectly guided to understand the manner of refusing love.

Such guidance can be accomplished only in an exchange between the educator and the child. The child is, as we have seen before, not learning from the educator but with the educator, the meaning of human actions. The child must be dependent and independent in learning this as in learning all else. The child cannot be left alone to search for meaningful relationships. The educator cannot spoil the child by refusing to contribute to this mentality, for then, the child would begin to build a structure of taboos for protection, and might eventually develop a super-ego far more tyrannical than the sternest parental authority. The book *The Lord of the Flies*, provides an example of the building of a taboo mentality without the guidance of adults.

Much as we would prefer to avoid mentioning sin, heaven, and hell to children who are still in a magical state of piety, we cannot. These words are in the children's vocabulary for one reason or another. They experience limitations, estrangements, chaos, bondage, disunity.

How are religious educators to speak to children about sin without fostering a taboo mentality? They must try to find authentic expressions both in words and gestures. Educators must examine the use of religious sentiment, the meaning of words for this affective time of learning, and the meaning of the sign of obtaining forgiveness: the sacrament of Penance.

SOME PRACTICAL SUGGESTIONS FOR THE GUIDANCE OF THE YOUNG CHILD

The Use of Religious Sentiment

An efficient and easy way to discipline children, or anyone for that matter, is to say that a given action is a sin. This makes God the jailor, the cop, the guard, the all-seeing eye, "Big Brother." Such discipline is no longer a possession of the growing personality but an imposition from outside—from someone transcendently, ominously outside. Discipline is the self-regulation of one's own behavior. To label certain actions "sinful" when the children are learning through their emotions (affectively), prepares them to respond in a negative, emotional way through fear.

It is unfair to children to have religious sentiment used to guide them in their growth. Children are at a magical stage of learning. Religion is not magical. All through history, science has helped to take away all superstitious trappings from the notion of religion. The religious experience occurs when a person identifies himself with a realization of transcendency.

This is why we wish to introduce children basic realities that can speak of God's presence with the language of the Bible. The language of the Bible is a poetry that respects the freedom of the person. It calls to individuals without manipulating them. It is this same respect with which we must work with the child. We cannot use religious sentiment to effect our deepest concern for young children—that they become able to answer freely to the call of the Father through Christ and his Spirit.

Thus, such phrases as, "You will make the baby Jesus (angels or Mary) cry if you do that," or even, "Now you are making God happy," imply a "Do-it-for-me" context that is asking for appeasement and not genuine commitment. Rather, we should speak of Jesus who loved his Father and went about doing good. We may remind a child of this responsibility by saying, "We don't do things like that in our house," and by saying it in a sympathetic tone of voice that tells the child that we understand. We should not place every act, from brushing teeth in the morning, to hanging up clothes in the evening, in the context of religion. Religion is not a transformed *Poor Richard's Almanac.* Religion is a personal relationship between God and human beings.

The Meaning of Words

It would be well, then, to examine not only the use of religious sentiment, but the meaning of some of the words in everyday language. To suggest a few, we may say that sin is a refusal to love. Hell is the loss of the chance to love. Forgiveness is reunion. We often ask children to say, "I'm sorry." How many times does the child hear, "I forgive you"? Should not the child hear and experience reunion in order to understand the meaning of the word? Confession is a time to demonstrate this reunion. Laws are helps to love. Christ is the law.

What about the old cliches: "Offer it up." "Make a good intention." "Deny yourself." Perhaps it is time to rethink these old saws, or say nothing at all. It is not that these words are no longer correct. They just seem to carry with them meanings no longer helpful. The child is concrete; our culture is concrete. When we offer something up we must see where and to whom. When we make a good intention we must know what it is about. The child is just finding an identity. Must the child deny that which he or she is finding? Further, a child understands what an adult is saying by the tone of voice used; the child will grow up and use the very same words.

The Meaning of the Sign of Obtaining Forgiveness

All that we have said so far is preparatory to understanding the sign, the sacrament of Penance. Before we speak of the ritual, let us mention that the immediate preparation is to understand other modes of asking forgiveness. In everyday life we seek reunion with our brothers and sisters. One of the best times for this is just before going to bed. Psychologists and neurologists say that bedtime is a time of regression, of thinking back over the day. A bedtime conversation could well be a time for asking forgiveness. Another time to ask forgiveness could be just before a main meal. The family is about to eat together. This is a time for union, joy, and love. One father told us that one night he came to the table to find the children pouting about some things that went wrong during the day. He thought of the meaning of the meal. (He was also a physician and was well aware of the physiological need for peace at mealtime.) He told the family that before they sat down to eat they should talk together about their troubles. They did and soon, quite spontaneously, they were saying, "I'm sorry," and "I forgive you."

Finally, children may learn to ask forgiveness in a conversation, with a gesture, or with a gift. The conversation could be informal or formal, in a group, or one to one. Perhaps an undramatic discussion of a problem which divides a family or a group is the best preparation for understanding the sign (sacrament) of reconciliation (penance). Such activity is sacramental. The work of Stephen Glen, Jane Nelson, and associates details these approaches in a completely "non-religious" context.

The ritual of asking forgiveness presupposes that one is aware of a need for reunion. This awareness has been spoken about traditionally as the examination of conscience. If lists of sins can be said to be more harmful than helpful, what can we ask ourselves? Perhaps we can help ourselves and our children to reflect on the meetings of the day. One can recall in the imagination all those encountered during the day and ask, "How have I given *and* received? How have I been open to others?" Without saying it directly we can help children to understand their relationships to others by helping them to ask themselves, "Remembering Christ, how have I loved others with my eyes, ears, mouth, hands, feet, and thoughts? How have I received love with my eyes, ears, mouth, hands, feet, and thoughts?"

Such considerations give us a formula for asking forgiveness.

I wish to thank God for
(*love received, love given*).
Even though God has been so good I
(*refused love*).

It may seem strange that we should mention what we have done that is good and, yet, is this not what St. Augustine did in his *Confessions?* When we see what we do as good and then say that it is possible because of God, then we see ourselves as we are before God. This positive approach can be said to resemble a technique that we use in the Montessori Method. When children are doing their work, the teacher notices the good things being done. The children reflect with the teacher and most often see what needs improvement. The formula above must not be considered as a necessity. Rather, it can be used as a question to get at the matter, much as we have other formulations such as, "How are you?"

The sacrament of Penance is a ritual in which a Christian publicly acknowledges the desire to be in union with all of humanity. The shape that the rite or formula takes to increase its clarity will depend not only on our own practice of asking forgiveness, but on our family and community practices of coming into reunion, of asking forgiveness of one another.

CONCLUSION

In the preceding paragraphs, we have asked, "Should we speak of the sacrament of Penance for the young child?" We proposed that this question can be answered only by priests, religious educators, and parents, who are directly involved with the child. We suggested that all three assume the role of religious educator at this time of personal growth. We also included some practical suggestions for the guidance of the young child. To contribute to this discussion, which should become an ever-increasing dialogue, we have offered some psychological, theological, and practical insights. The answer to the what, where, when, and how of confession for the young child can be decided when these and other insights are considered in relationship to the child within his particular Christian community.

SUGGESTED READINGS

Books

Monden, Louis. *Sin, Liberty and Law.* New York: Sheed and Ward, 1965. (See especially Chapter 1.)

Nelson, Jane. *Positive Discipline.* New York: Ballantine Books, 1987.

Oraison, Marc. *Love or Constraint?* Glenrock, N. I., Paulist Press, (Deus) 1961. (See especially Chapter 5.)

Stern, Karl. *The Third Revolution.* New York: Doubleday, (Image), 1961. (See especially Chapter 5.)

Appendix II
The Preschool Religion Class

Since this work was begun, there has been a growing interest in applying the ideas that have been experimented with, and that are contained in this book, to preschool classes. In various parishes where parents have become more and more involved in preparing their children for First Communion, and where, consequently, it has been seen that the present Sunday Mass is not the best experience for the young child, there has been interest in having a preschool class conducted while parents are at Mass. Probably the greatest interest for preschool religion classes is expressed by those parents whose children are not able to go to parochial schools. Since the experiment we undertook began within a Montessori classroom, it can be applied to a classroom situation.

ADVANTAGES OF THE FORMAL CLASSROOM

Undoubtedly the greatest advantage of the formal classroom situation is that experiences such as we have suggested can be shared by more children. This group sharing is helpful to the individual child. It is good for children to hear what their peers have to say about their own experiences, and each is, of course, enriched by the presence. All of the others that we have suggested so far, then, can be used profitably in a preschool religion class as well as in the home.

In the Montessori classrooms where this experiment was conducted, the children had an average of one group lesson each week. Of course, the children were in an environment rich with possibilities for incidental, on-the-spot teaching. We noticed that even in Montessori classrooms which did not attempt formal religious education, the presence of small baskets of shells, rocks, or crystals still provided an opportunity for religious education. In fact, in any classroom where a child is taught to reverence themselves, the things with which they work, and the people with whom they work, there is the possibility for religious education.

Many teachers of primary grades have used these lessons as supplementary to their text, and, in some cases, have used this material exclusively. Some of them report that they have one lesson or experience each week and that during the rest of the week they looked for opportune times to prepare for this experience. Some teachers of intermediate and upper grades, and even of high school classes, have adapted the lessons and have presented the same basic symbols to their classes. We would suggest that these teachers first experience the meaning of the sign and then present it to the children as they have understood it. This may seem difficult, but is not if teachers realize that all they are doing is sharing an experience with a class with which they are constantly working.

REQUIREMENTS FOR THE CLASSROOM

For a teacher of preschoolers or school-age children who plans to use the lessons in this book, we have a few suggestions concerning setting up and presenting of the exercises. First, be sure that the materials used are artistic and in good taste. This is the reason we have used so many natural symbols. Second, set aside a special place in your classroom to store these things. Small trays for the shells and rocks, for example, not only enhance the articles as a frame does a picture, but they mark out a space where these things can be placed. Montessori speaks about "sacred space." Reverence, demonstrated by care and respect, is the key concept here. Some of the articles will be placed according to their function. We do not feel that there should be a special "religion corner." However, the most special place should be reserved for the Bible—after the children have been introduced to it.

THE PRESCHOOL RELIGION TEACHER

If you are concerned about setting up a preschool class, then we suggest that you try to combine in your classes two-and-a-half, three-, four-, and five-year-olds. This is a more natural grouping of children than you would have if the three-, four-, and five-year-olds were separated. This more natural grouping means that each age group can help the others. The younger children can help the older ones to feel that sense of wonder that they may have already lost or that was never cultivated. Children of the same family can be in the same classroom, sharing an experience together that they can then bring home. In some places the teachers teach only for a part of the year in order that the work be shared by different persons. This is understandable. However, we urge that the children have the same teacher throughout the year, because a continuity of experience is ensured only through a continuity of identification with the same person.

The teacher must spend time in preparing lesson plans. Since each parish, community, region has its own unique personality, its own particular needs, teachers can be successful only where they have the opportunity to get together and rewrite lesson plans. One teacher cannot make lesson plans for another teacher. She or he can merely present the truth experienced and then give some of the theory involved. The teacher who borrows lesson plans must be able to adapt them. For the busy mother who is the teacher of the preschool class this suggestion may seem frightening, but there are few alternatives. We can say, though, that those mothers who have been working with preschool children and who have had to meet with other teachers and prepare their own lessons have been so enriched by this sharing that they felt that the time was well spent. Perhaps this was the way the first Christians communicated their understanding of their experience.

If teachers prepare together in this way, their own creativity extends each of these ideas into several lesson plans. We do not, therefore, suggest that each lesson plan be used and then dropped. First, children of this age love to repeat the same lesson or experience. Second, the variations of the central activities indicated in each chapter have a deepening effect upon the child. One could, moreover, extend the Christmas tree lesson to a Valentine tree, an Easter egg tree, or a family tree. In one instance, children worked with finger paints and then experienced water as they washed their hands. The children held their hands over a basin while another poured water over them to clean them.

The teacher's preparation should include some time spent in parental involvement. In some places, the only children who may participate in the preschool class are those whose parents come to regular meetings to hear about what the children are learning. In other places, a celebration is held with both parents and children participating. The children share with their parents an experience of light, for example, by lighting candles with them and singing the songs they have learned in class. Elsewhere, children are taught while their parents are having a discussion in another classroom. Here, the children wake up in the morning and remind their parents, "We go to class tonight!" The children experience water at the same time that their parents are discussing the meaning of water in the Old Testament.

In most places teachers write letters to be taken home to the parents. The more personal and informal these letters are, the greater the parental involvement. When parents are not involved with what is going on in the preschool class, there seems to be little reason to expect that the children will have any real religious education. The four-year-old girl reflects her parents' attitude. Since we are preeminently concerned with attitudes, we cannot overlook parental involvement.

If you are a teacher of a preschool class, have open shelves holding all materials needed for such activities as drawing, cutting, and pasting. In many places where there are preschool classes, this is impossible because the teachers are using other teachers' classrooms or are holding classes in a church basement. In places where a permanent classroom cannot be found, set the materials out the evening before. This is part of teacher preparation. Children should have their own shoe boxes, which contain the needed materials, and which may be taken out before they come to class, and put away in a closet afterwards. This arrangement, however, diminishes the child's mobility. In other words, there is little opportunity for a successful cycle of activity. The ideal situation is to have open shelves. On these shelves there should be small trays that the children can pick up. They could then arrange on them a scissors, a piece of paper, some crayons, and other materials needed for their work. This provides for economy of movement and helps the children to organize their activities properly. The teacher should not have to go to a cupboard and get something each time a child needs it. Nor should a teacher have to stand in front of the group passing out the materials. Such assembly line procedures are not consonant in an age where we have learned to act in a more patterned response. Marshall McLuhan and others who have given us insight into communication arts, tell us that we are being formed to respond to patterns rather than to linear movement, such as we received formerly from the printed page. In other words, perhaps a new approach to work is coming that will make the assembly line obsolete.

Perhaps one of the most important aids in getting children to work independently and satisfactorily is to help them learn through a series of preliminary lessons how to get materials, use them, and replace them. This means that the first two months of a preschool class may be spent helping the children to understand how they will work within the environment of their classroom. This does not mean that they will do nothing except learn how to use materials. But most of their time will be spent in this way and will be ended with some kind of group activity such as a song or a story. Two months or eight Sundays of this kind of lesson is not a waste—it is the best preparation for helping the children to work on their own. This, in turn, enables the teacher to work one-to-one with a child. We suggest that the children have, for example, a lesson in pasting. The teacher should demonstrate slowly, step-by-step, what the children should do when they want to paste. The children should be grouped about the teacher as they learn how to get material needed for pasting. The teacher should then let the children take turns getting the tray, placing the paste in a little dish with a stick, taking a piece of paper, and perhaps a scissor. Children love to demonstrate in this way. They learn best through demonstration. These first eight weeks can be seen as well spent when one thinks of the advantage of teaching children to carefully use the signs of their environment. Again, reverence is the key concept.

SCHEDULE FOR A PRESCHOOL RELIGION CLASS

We suggest that a preschool class of one hour use a schedule similar to the following:

15 min. 1. When the children arrive, greet them cordially. This is not time lost. Arrival and departure times are important for all people, but most important for the small child who needs to feel welcome and needs to be able to say goodbye. The manner in which we say "hello" and "goodbye" is an index to the manner in which we relate to people. Children may want to talk to others about what has happened since they were last in school, or they may wish to watch the fish swimming, and so forth. This gives the teacher a chance to observe the children. Then, allow them to choose their own activities.

15 min. 2. Gather the children to present the lesson, or give it to a small group. The whole group may not be interested.

15 min. 3. The children may now work on an activity related to the lesson. We have found that it is good to give children an activity to do first and then gather them in a small group to talk about what they have done. The sense of discovery is better achieved in this way. For example, children may make decorations for a Valentine tree and then come together around a branch in a pot of clay, and, one by one, as they are called, hang the decorations on it. Then, too, there can be some valentines under the tree that can be given out. This kind of activity may be called a culminating experience.

15 min. 4. The children may either play together or go outside for activities that involve physical exercise.

Additional 5. If possible, have juice and cookies together.
Time

THE CLASSROOM SETTING

As we mentioned earlier, the classroom may have to be in a church basement or it may belong to another teacher. Whatever the conditions, it should be possible at times for the children to be together in a circle either on a rug or on chairs. There should be enough space for the children to work in, for a crowded situation militates against order and peace. Class size should be dictated by the size of the room. We know of one place where there is one teacher for every twelve children, and where each teacher has an assistant. This means that there are two adults to every twelve children. The assistant is a high school girl who has volunteered her help. Such an assistant can be invaluable in working quietly with the children, and can also serve as another person with whom the children can identify.

Perhaps the most important aspect of any formal or informal learning situation, especially at this age, is a resolve on the part of the teacher not to be concerned about the amount of information the children are getting, but rather about the quality of the experience. One teacher friend wrote a poem (unpublished) about this kind of education of the young child. The final words of the poem are:

> If all that is life in him
> Is glad of the living—
> What has he yet to learn?
>
> —*G. Ellen Lorts*

The religious experiences of the young child will have a lasting impression. They will bear out Montessori's words: "There are moments of happiness given to man that he may continue his existence in peace."

SUGGESTED READING

Book

McLuhan, Herbert Marshall. *Understanding Media.* New York: McGraw-Hill, 1964.

Appendix III
The Mentally Challenged and
Non-English Speaking Child

RELIGION, MONTESSORI AND THE MENTALLY CHALLENGED

It is interesting to note that Maria Montessori began her work with small children by working with the mentally deficient, or what we today call the mentally challenged, or exceptional child. This is where she found, through the works of others, certain pieces of apparatus that were developed to help the mentally challenged to learn. Anyone working with such individuals gets a better understanding of how the average personality operates and so it was significant that Maria Montessori based her whole method for children on techniques she developed while working with these challenging children.

This has significance for religious education. Because some human beings come to be interested in materials and ideas that are simply lower in scale of sophistication, it may take them longer to go from one idea to another. It also means that this person needs more attention from the teacher. As Dr. Thomas J. Banta says in a chapter in a book called *Training the Developmentally Young* "... 'retarded' and 'normal' are, in a sense, then, inappropriate labels. All are members of the same species; all exist on the same continuum; the differences are a matter of degree."

Montessori felt that the problems of these mentally challenged children were more pedagogical then medical, a point that is very much mirrored in modern psychological thought. If this is so, those working with special children can become, in the process, excellent teachers, because they are forced to look slowly at each step in their presentation and approach.

In the preparation of this book, I came in contact with a group of people in Chicago who were working with mentally challenged children. They were using the work of Father Jean Mesny, Ph.D., who has been working with special children in France, but they were translating his work in more than one way. I had an opportunity to speak with this team of people and received an unpublished manuscript outlining their approach. The fact that this team and I were heading for the same goal, not knowing about each others' efforts, was astounding.

The main approach of this team of people and my work was almost exactly the same. In each case, the child was being given some object that would fascinate and could symbolize by sheer esthetic attractiveness something that was transcendent. Dr. Mesny had an occasion to visit one of the schools that was experimenting with this work. He told the teachers that they should slow down the approach by putting into the environment a rock, water, growing seeds, stalks of wheat, and other objects, and letting the child slowly relate to them, even before making any presentation about them. There is no doubt that Father Mesny was making this suggestion because of his own experiments with mentally challenged children. The suggestion was an excellent one, and the teachers began to leave things around in the classroom before they even made any formal presentation based on them.

Others who have worked with these special children have used the lessons in this book with success. The caution here is to repeat, prolong, and slow down the presentation. Other than that, the very same objects can be used and the same concepts can be discovered, even though in a lesser degree of sophistication. The emotional content of the exercises presented here are attractive to a child who relies more on emotive than cognitive sensibilities.

At the same time that I was encountering people who were working with the mentally challenged, I had occasion to work for three weeks with lay volunteers who trained in San Antonio, Texas, to work with Spanish-speaking children. As the lessons were presented to them, the students kept asking how this could be done with non-English-speaking children, particularly because these lay volunteers could not speak Spanish. The lay volunteers were not only taking theoretical courses, but they were also working with the children at the same time.

First of all, the volunteers had to learn the cardinal principle of this book: that a symbol has no particular tongue. A symbol that is archetypal speaks to all people at all times in all ages. Small children force one to find this kind of symbol simply because they start out life being nonverbal. As soon as the students began to realize this fact, they themselves, made lesson plans using this principle.

Consequently, they came back terribly excited the day they used candles with the Mexican children. The awe, excitement, and communication of something transcendent spoke more than any language could ever hold. They were able to pray with them and speak of hope and of the risen Lord in this very simple way. A lesson was developed on the spot, using some of the pomegranates that were ripe that hot August. The children saw that the many seeds made one pomegranate. This was a very organic and real symbol to these children who could reach up to the trees and pluck a fruit that spoke of such richness, not only to them in our times, but in the Old Testament as well. It is then without hesitation that I recommend the exercises of this book to those working with non-English-speaking children.

Bibliography

BOOKS

Berne, Eric. *Games People Play*. New York: Grove Press, 1964.

Berryman, Jerome W. and Sonja M. Stewart. *Young Children and Worship*. Louisville: Westminster John Knox Press, 1989.

Bowlby, John. *Child Care and the Growth of Love*. Balfimore, MD: Penguin Books, 1953.

Bruner, Jerome S. *The Process of Education*. New York: Vintage, 1960.

—— *Toward a Theory of Instruction*. Cambridge, Mass.: Belknap Press, 1966.

Campbell, Joseph. *Myths to Live By*. New York: Bantam Books, 1988.

Cavalletti, Sofia, et al. *The Good Shepherd and the Child*. Chicago: Liturgy Training Publications, 1992.

——*The Religious Potential of the Child*. Chicago: Liturgy Training Publications, 1992.

Coles, Robert. *The Spiritual Life of Children*. Boston: Houghton Mifflin, 1990.

——The Moral Intelligence of Children. New York: Random House, 1997.

Danielou, Jean. *God and the Ways of Knowing*. New York: Meridian Books, 1962.

DeLenval, H. Lubienska. *The Whole Man at Worship*. New York: Desclee Co., 1961.

Dreikurs, Rudolf. *Psychology in the Classroom*. New York: Harper & Row, 1957.

Durwell, Francis X. *The Resurrection*. New York: Sheed & Ward, 1960.

Eliade, Mircea. *Images and Symbols*. New York: Sheed & Ward, 1960.

Eliade, M. and Kitagawa, J. M. *The History of Religions*. Chicago: Univ. of Chicago Press, 1959.

—— *Cosmos and History*. Torch Books, Harper, New York 1965.

Erickson, Erik. *Childhood and Society*. New York: W. W. Norton and Co., 1963.

Farges, Marie. *Our Children and the Lord*. Notre Dame, Ind.: Fides, 1965.

Flavell, J. H. *The Developmental Psychology*. Princeton, N.J.: D.Van Nostrand, 1963.

Fromm, Eric. *The Art of Loving*. New York: Bantam, 1962.

Getman, C. N., and Kane, Elmer R. *The Physiology of Readiness*. Minneapolis: P.A.S.S., 1964. (See especially the Overview.)

Ginott, Haim C. *Between Parent and Child*. New York: Macmillan, 1965.

Gobbi, Gianna. *Feed My Lambs/Montessori Principles Applied to the Catechesis of Children*. New York: Random House, 1997.

Harris, Maria. *Dance of the Spirit*. New York: Bantam Books, 1988.

Heller, Robert. *The Children's God*. Chicago: University of Chicago Press, 1986.

Hoffman, Edward. *Visions of Innocence: Spiritual and Inspirational Experiences of Childhood*. Boston: Shambhala/Random House, 1992.

Jersild, Arthur T. *When Teachers Face Themselves*. New York: Teachers College Press, 1955.

Jung, Carl G. *Man and His Symbols*. New York: Doubleday, 1964.

Kellog, Rhoda and O'Dell, Scott. *CRM*. New York: Random House Publication, 1967.

Langer, Suzanne. *Philosophy in a New Key*. New York: New American Library, 1965.

Lee, R. S. *Your Growing Child and Religion*. New York: Macmillan, 1963.

LeFebvre, S. and Perin, L. *Bringing Your Child to God*. New York: P. J. Kenedy & Son, 1963.

Lindbergh, Ann Morrow. *Gift from the Sea*. New York: Vintage, 1955.

Menninger, M. D. Karl. *Love Against Hate*. New York: Harvest, 1942.

Monden, Louis. *Sin, Liberty and Law*. New York: Sliced & Ward, 1965.

Montessori, Maria. *Montessori Method*. New York: Schocken, 1964.

—— *Dr. Montessori's Own Handbook*. New York: Schocken, 1965.

——*Discovery of the Child*. India: Kelakshetre Publications 1962.

—— *Absorbent Mind*. India: Theosophical Publishing House 1961.

——*Spontaneous Activity in Education*. Cambridge, Mass: Robert Bentley, 1964.

Myers, Barbara Kimes and William. *Engaging in Transcendence/The Church's Ministry and Covenant with Young Children*. Cleveland: The Pilgrm Press, 1992.

Nelson, Gertrud Mueller. *To Dance with God: Family Ritual and Community Celebration*. New York: Paulist Press, 1986.

Nelson, Jane. *Positive Discipline*. New York: Ballantine Books, 1987.

Oraison, Marc. *Love or Constraint?* New York: Deus 1961.

Otto, Rudolf. *The Idea of the Holy*. New York: Oxford Press, 1964.

Paley, Vivian Gussin. *The Boy Who Would Be a Helicopter*. Cambridge: Harvard University Press, 1992.

——*You Can't Say You Can't Play*. Cambridge: Harvard University Press, 1992.

Parsch, Pius, Dr. *The Church's Year of Grace*. Collegeville, Minn.: Liturgical Press, 1962.

Pines, Maya. *Revolution in Learning*. New York: Harper & Row, 1966.

Pipher, Mary. *The Shelter of Each Other*. New York: Ballantine Books, 1997.

Pottebaum, Gerard A. *To Walk with a Child*. Loveland, Ohio: Treehaus Communications, Inc., 1993.

——*A Child Shall Lead Them*. Loveland, Ohio: Treehaus Communications, Inc., 1992.

Rambusch, Nancy McCormick. *Learning How to Learn*. Baltimore, Md.: Helicon, 1963.

Robinson, John S. T. *The New Reformation*. Philadelphia: Westminster Press, 1965.

Schillebeeckx, E., 0. P. *Christ the Sacrament of the Encounter With God*. New York: Sheed & Ward, 1964.

Searle, Mark. *The Church Speaks about Sacraments with Children*. Chicago: Liturgy Training Publications, 1990.

Stern, Karl. *The Third Revolution*. New York: Doubleday (Image), 1961.

Wann, Kenneth D., et. al. *Fostering Intellectual Development in Young Children*. New York: Columbia University Press, 1929.

Weber, Hans-Ruedi. *Jesus and the Children*. Loveland, Ohio: Treehaus Communications, Inc., 1993.

Whitehead, A. N. *The Aims of Education and Other Essays*. New York: Macmillan, 1959.

ARTICLES

Gelineau, Joseph, S. J. "The Nature and Role of Signs in the Economy of the Covenant" *Worship*, Vol 39, No.9, Nov.1965, pp. 530–550.

Leonard, Augusfine, 0. P. "Human Religious Development of the Child," *Lumen Vitae*, 1957, #2.

Mead, Margaret "Ritual Expression of the Cosmic Sense." WORSHIP, Vol. 40, No.2, Feb.1966. pp. 66–72.

Pohier, Jacques M., 0. P. "Religious Mentality and Child Mentality." *Lumen Vitae*, Studies in Religious Psychology II, 1961, pp. 21–44.

Schillebeeckx, E. 0. P. "Transubstantiation, Transfiguration, and Transignification," *Worship*, Vol. 40, No.6, June, 1966.

About the Author

In 1966, Jeannine Schmid directed The Montessori Center Rooms, Inc., preschools for lower-income families of inner-city areas in Cincinnati, Ohio. In 1981, she cofounded and directed the Laureate Private School for Toddlers to Eighth Grade in San Luis Obispo, California.

She taught a course entitled "Religious Education and the Montessori Method" for the Religious Educational Institute held at Mundelein College and the Loyola University Pastoral Institute, Chicago, and for Manhattan College in New York. From 1972 to 1992 she taught undergraduate and graduate courses in child development and psychology.

Dr. Schmid's introduction to the Montessori approach began in 1962. Studying under Mrs. Nancy McCormick Rambusch, she received certification as a preschool Montessori teacher and then taught in a Montessori school in Oak Park, Illinois, for one year. At that time, she began experimenting with the teaching of religion using this new educational approach. In 1966, she completed work on a Masters Degree in Theology at Marquette University under Bernard Cooke, applying the theoretical principles of modern theology to this new pedagogy. In 1972, she completed studies for a Ph.D. from Purdue University in child development and family life.